A

REVOLUTIONARY

MYSTERY

A REVOLUTIONARY MYSTERY

An Exegetical Commentary on
First Corinthians Two

BY
SPIROS ZODHIATES, TH.D.

AMG
PUBLISHERS
Chattanooga, TN 37422

A Revolutionary Mystery

An Exegetical Commentary on
First Corinthians Two

ISBN 0-89957-507-1

Printed in the United States of America
02 01 00 99 98 97 –R– 6 5 4 3 2 1

To my only son, Philip, who made my heart rejoice through his choice to serve the Living Christ.

Contents

Preface

Do you wish you could understand God better? So do I. And yet, if we could fully understand Him, it would mean bringing Him down to our level. Then He would cease to be a God worthy of our worship and adoration.

Why does God hide certain of His secrets and ways from us? Is it for our good? Is such a partial revelation of Himself for our glory? The second chapter of First Corinthians says it is.

In this book I have endeavored to expound from Scripture the "whys" and "hows" of the mysteriousness of God and His dealings with us. Understanding this great chapter of the Bible will give you greater insight into this matter, as it has me. This book was written for that purpose. May it prove of comfort and help to you in dealing with the perplexities of life.

SPIROS ZODHIATES

An Overview of First Corinthians

Author: Paul the apostle, author of thirteen other epistles to various individuals and congregations.

Date: About A.D. 55.

Recipients: The congregation Paul had established in Corinth.

Place: From Ephesus

Theme: Paul had received news about the Corinthian brethren from several sources (1 Cor. 1:11; 7:1; 16:17). The church was afflicted with many of the problems that face young churches and new converts. The apostle, under the inspiration of the Holy Spirit, decided to write this urgent letter to admonish and instruct the church. Among other topics he discussed: the necessity of church discipline (5:1–13); divisions and disputes among Christians (1:10–16; 6:1–11); matters of conscience (8:1–13; 10:19–33); the support of preachers (9:1–27); abuses of the Lord's Supper (10:16–17, 21; 11:17–34); the misuse of spiritual gifts (12:1—14:40); and the importance of the resurrection of Jesus Christ (15:1–58).

An Outline of First Corinthians

In the days of the apostle Paul, Corinth was the capital city of the Roman province of Achaia and the glory of Greece. Though its great ancient splendor had been destroyed by the Romans in 120 B.C., the city was rebuilt under Julius Caesar and restored to wealth and luxury under Augustus. Among all the cities of the world, however, it was most well known for its lewdness. The apostle Paul lived in Corinth for eighteen months (Acts 18:11). After his departure, Paul went to Ephesus. During his three-year stay there, he heard reports of wickedness and division within the Corinthian church. In an effort to correct these evils, Paul wrote several letters to them, including the epistle of First Corinthians.

1:1–9	The introductory remarks of Paul.
1:10–16	Paul condemns the divisions in the church and exhorts its members to unity.
1:17—2:16	Paul defends his ministry. He has preached the wisdom of Christ crucified. This wisdom is foolishness to the world, but is the glory of all those to whom the Spirit of God has revealed the truthfulness of it.
3:1–5	Paul declares that the simplicity of his teaching was due to the carnal state of the Corinthians, which state is clearly evidenced by their divisions.
3:6–23	Jesus Christ is the only foundation. Ministers are mere servants; the work is God's.
4:1–6	The duty of ministers is faithfulness.
4:6–21	Paul contrasts the arrogance and conceit of the false teachers to the humility and sacrifice of the apostles. Using his unique position as their spiritual father, Paul calls on the Corinthian believers to be discerning.
5:1–13	Flagrant, sexual immorality was being practiced by one of the members of the congregation. Paul reproves

1 Cor. 2:1 | *Preaching Christ Crucified*

And I, brethren, when I came to you, came not with excellency of speech or of wisdom, declaring unto you the testimony of God.

The First Concern of a Preacher

Two young men broke into a photo studio one Sunday night. They murdered the aged owner and robbed the cash drawer. Headlines of the crime appeared on the front page of Monday morning's papers. The two youths had been apprehended and charged with murder. Because their names seemed familiar to the secretary of a local church, she looked them up in the visitors' book. Sure enough, they had attended the church on Sunday morning and that night they committed murder! The pastor's subject that morning had been "An Educated Ministry." Only God knows what the end result might have been if the minister had preached on Christ's power to save and to change sinful hearts.

Preachers today would do well to emulate the example of the apostle Paul, who was saved himself by the cross of Christ and determined to make it the central theme of his preaching. From our studies in the first chapter of Paul's first epistle to the Corinthians, we learned some fundamental facts about the character of the Corinthians and Paul. First, the Corinthians were prone to attach themselves to individual preachers and forget the central character of their faith, the Lord Jesus Christ. Second, they concerned themselves with minor doctrines such as baptism, while neglecting the gospel's central theme, the cross of Christ. Third, they tended to be drawn toward philosophical speculation, failing to see that the gospel was the power of God unto salvation while at the same time fully satisfying to the enlightened mind of the believer.

Where Paul himself was concerned, he demonstrated to the Corinthians that he was saved and was henceforth committed to putting first things first in his ministry. He was a very capable man who knew how to choose his priorities. He demonstrated through his ministry in Corinth that a preacher ought never to accommodate himself to the unwise desires of the people he is trying to reach, but should seek to meet their spiritual needs.

Paul apparently was an intellectual man who might have been greatly tempted to show that he was one-up on the intellectual Corinthians. Thus he would receive their acclaim. But Christ had definitely subdued this desire in him. When he became a Christian, he learned to give priority to what would meet the need of every sinner—the preaching of Christ crucified.

Not that Paul could not speak on philosophical and social issues. He did tackle these in the course of his ministry, but they were not his primary concern. What is the use of teaching a man not to steal, or not to dishonor his body through fornication, when he possesses a sinful nature whose natural inclination is to sin? Our first concern should be to get people saved, to bring them into the sphere of Christ, and then all these other matters can be brought to their attention.

Paul was a man of clear goals and purposes. He therefore used his talents to preach on the subjects that would accomplish these goals. If you want a man to stop stealing, and he is unregenerated, you do not preach honesty to him but the need of salvation of his entire being. Stealing is only a propensity of his sinful nature.

These considerations are necessary if we are to understand what Paul says in chapter two, which begins, "And I having come to you, brethren, come not with the superiority of expressed intelligence or of wisdom, declaring to you the testimony of God."

Observe again that he never failed to call them "brethren," in spite of the fact that he had to admonish them. He believed that as his brethren in Christ they were entitled to the rationale of his behavior among them. They knew that Paul was capable of excellent speech and reasoning. In fact, when Luke described Paul's activity in the Corinthian synagogues when he had first come to Corinth, he said, "And he reasoned [*dielegeto*] in the synagogue every Sabbath, and persuaded the Jews and the Greeks" (Acts 18:4). From that word *dielegeto* we derive our English word "dialectics." It is akin to *logou* in 1 Corinthians 2:1. In Acts 17:2 exactly the same word (*dielegeto*) is used to describe the manner of Paul's ministry in the synagogue in Athens.

But how can we reconcile Luke's statement—that Paul reasoned in the synagogue and persuaded both Jews and Greeks—with Paul's statement in 1 Corinthians 2:1 that he "came not in the superiority of word and wisdom declaring unto [the Corinthians] the testimony of God"? Of course one must use reason in speaking, and Paul used it everywhere. It would be wrong to rely on human reasoning alone to achieve God's ends. Paul was a very clever man, who made good use of his native keen intelligence. Just read the chapters in the Acts that describe man's efforts to persecute and kill Paul, and note how he brought forth every possible intelligent opposition.

In Acts 21:37, out of nowhere Paul began to speak Greek to the chief captain, completely astonishing him. "Canst thou speak Greek?" he asked. And then in verse 39 Paul said, "I am a man which am a Jew of Tarsus, a city in Cilicia, a citizen of no mean city: and, I beseech thee, suffer me to speak unto the people." Read how he handled the Pharisees, setting them in opposition to the Sadducees by saying, "Men and brethren, I am a Pharisee, the son of a Pharisee" (Acts 23:6). He so dexterously handled the situation that he gained the support of the Pharisees, which he desperately needed at that critical time. Indeed, the Pharisees were the ones who said, "We find no evil in this man" (Acts 23:9). When he was about to be scourged by the Roman soldiers, he turned to the centurion and said, "Is it lawful for you to scourge a man that is a Roman, and uncondemned?" (Acts 22:25). This was a masterful, extremely intelligent handling of a series of most difficult situations. That was Paul for you, equal to every difficulty.

Paul was a learned man. He had been a student of the rabbinical school of Gamaliel in Jerusalem (Acts 22:3) and had been promoted in it, as he himself says in Galatians 1:14, above many his own age. No reader of his epistles can be unaware of the use he made of this learning. In fact, many readers may sympathize with what Peter says about Paul's writings, that perhaps because of Paul's erudition he writes some things that are hard to understand (2 Pet. 3:16).

But not only did Paul have the learning that the schools could give, he also had the culture that comes from extensive travel and contact with men of different nationalities and occupations. As a public speaker he was not inferior to any of the apostles. If you compare the speeches of Peter and Paul reported in the Acts, I think you will find those of Paul more comprehensive in matter and more versatile in method. They disclose in a high degree the public speaker's grasp of local circumstances and the varying moods and attitudes of the audience.

Therefore we must conclude as a general principle that Paul not only was an extremely intelligent and capable man, but also that he used his mind to its fullest God-given potentiality. Mary D. James, in her hymn "All for Jesus," echoes the spirit of Paul when she says that she dedicates to the Lord "All my being's ransomed powers." That is what Paul did, and that is what we must do if we are to be effective Christian witnesses in our own sphere of influence.

How to Present the Truth of the Gospel

Two errors need to be refuted in man's thinking about human intelligence. The first is that unaided reason is sufficient to solve his basic needs and the problems of the world in general. The second is that the Christian believer should not use his reason to solve his difficulties or attempt to serve his Lord, but should expect some mystical guidance from above in every situation.

Moreover, we must not conclude from 1 Corinthians 2:1 that human wisdom or innate intelligence is to be despised. These are useful in their realm. There is a place where we must speak of the reasonableness of the gospel. We must show that, to become a Christian, man does not need to bury his intelligence but to use it. But while human reason has its own realm and usefulness, the gospel makes us realize the limitations of that reason. When it comes to the origin of all things, to the sustenance of our world, to the human soul, to the mystery of the human predicament, to death, to man's sinfulness and what to do about it, to the great hereafter, man's reason can only say, "I do not know."

The apostle Paul appealed to reason. He constantly started the presentation of the gospel with the historical person of the Lord Jesus Christ, saying in effect, "What are you reasonable men going to do with Him? He rose from the dead. Therefore He is entitled to be believed when He tells you of things which your mind has proved incapable of solving." What is 1 Corinthians 15 but the greatest argument for the historicity and the practical accomplishments of the resurrection? No mental lightweight wrote that chapter. And it was written to the Corinthians.

No, Paul did not scoff at the skillful presentation of higher truths to men. In fact, he always adapted his teachings to those whom he taught and to the circumstances in which he taught. Therefore, when he says that he did not come with wisdom of words, it should not be understood as being a general fling at rhetorical or oratorical modes of handling the truth. Rather it should be understood as making the implication that there are some things which the most skillful oratory cannot touch, that there are deeper truths, higher realms, than any which can be reached by rhetoric.

What Paul is declaring is that, no matter how eloquently the gospel is presented, we must remember that it is the crucified Christ and the simple proclamation of the fact of Christ's substitutionary death that can attract the sinner and save him.

"I come not in the superiority of word, utterance (*logou*), or wisdom," he says. That is as literal a translation as I can give you. "Superiority" (or "excellency," as it is translated in the Authorized Version) is *huperochē* in Greek. This noun is found only here and in 1 Timothy 2:2 (where it is translated "authority"). As a verb it is found in Romans 13:1, Philippians 2:3; 3:8; 4:7, and 1 Peter 2:13. It is a compound word made up of *huper*, meaning "over," and *echō*, meaning "have." *Huperechō*, which is still used commonly in modern Greek, means "to have it over" someone, as we would say in slang, "to be superior to." It clearly brings two persons or groups into focus—those above and those below; or something that stands above and superior to another. I think it is misleading to translate the word in 1 Corinthians 2:1 "excellency." Look at it: "I . . . came not with excellency of speech or of wisdom." Immediately you conclude that Paul is attacking the value of speech and wisdom, when in reality he is not attacking them as such. What he declares is that they are not superior to something else—which is the content of the gospel, Christ crucified.

Paul was a born orator and logician, but he wanted to impress on the Corinthians that natural abilities must take a secondary place. They do not "have it over" the plain truth of the gospel, which is that Christ was crucified for our sins. The moral for all of us, then, is that we are to use our abilities fully, but with humility, recognizing that they are God-given. This should apply in all fields of legitimate endeavor. If you are a physician, for instance, remember that your skill is needed, but in the final analysis, it is God who has the upper hand. Healing comes from the Lord: "I am the Lord that healeth thee" (Ex. 15:26). "Bless the Lord, O my soul, and forget not all his benefits: who forgiveth all thine iniquities; who healeth all thy diseases" (Ps. 103:2, 3). But that does not mean that a physician ought not to use all his medical knowledge and skill. He should, but he must not place them first in the healing process.

The same is true of the ministry. Use your abilities, preacher, but do not think that they are what will bring souls to Christ. If you do not clearly present the gospel, but simply seek to show off your natural abilities, do not expect to see lives changed. You may attract the admiration of men but there will be no conversions. As Luther aptly said, "He preaches best who aims at being understood rather than being admired." And someone else observed, "The Christian pulpit needs to be on guard against the snare of words. One of the greatest curses that can come to a young preacher is a glib tongue. It means almost certain ruin. How futile, no matter how pleasing, are the efforts of a ministerial rhetorician."

William Cowper has set down in poetry the qualifications of a preacher of which he thinks Paul would approve. He says,

> Would I describe a preacher such as Paul,
> Were he on earth, would hear, approve, and own—
> Paul should himself direct me. I would trace
> His master-strokes, and draw from his design.
> I would express him simple, grave, sincere;
> In doctrine, uncorrupt; in language, plain;
> And plain in manner; decent, solemn, chaste,
> And natural in gesture; much impressed
> Himself, as conscious of his awful charge,
> And anxious mainly that the flock he feeds
> May feel it too. Affectionate in look,
> And tender in address, as well becomes
> A messenger of grace to guilty men.

Transmitting God's Message Faithfully

Every man in the public eye has his critics, no matter how faithfully he tries to do what is right. It is quite possible that in the church in Corinth there was a group of critics opposed to Paul. In spite of the fact that he used his God-given natural abilities to proclaim the gospel, he apparently did not desire to display his oratorical and intellectual powers to their full extent. Or perhaps it was just that his critics would have liked less gospel and more oratory and philosophy.

This is probably why Paul seems apologetic about a certain lack of boldness in speaking to the Corinthians. No other church seems to have made it the subject of comment, for all the references to it occur in the Corinthian letters (1 Cor. 2:1, 4; 2 Cor. 3:12; 10:10; 11:6). Do not forget that Corinth was a place where factions developed easily. Some sided with Paul, others with Apollos, and still others with Peter. The criticism of Paul demonstrated the attitude of one section of the congregation.

With regard to Apollos, we know that he succeeded Paul in Corinth. We are told that he was an Alexandrian by birth, and "an eloquent man" (Acts 18:24). His possession of this gift in an exceptional degree would naturally attract attention in a community like Corinth, although it made them indifferent to his other outstanding abilities such as: his weight of biblical learning, his fervor of spirit, his exact scholarship, and his dialectical skill, all of which are mentioned along with his eloquence in the same section of Acts (18:24–28).

We can see how superficial was the judgment of those Corinthians who found in the eloquence of Apollos the basis for their criticism of Paul, the man who had established the church in their city. Compared, however, with his other gifts, which Paul also had in no mean degree, the eloquence of Apollos was indeed something to be grateful for, but it had no value in itself. Paul did not make the mistake of underestimating the gift that the Corinthians had obviously over-estimated. His object rather was to correct the false emphasis put upon it, and to remove the source of one of those divisions in the Church that were weakening the unity of its testimony and work (Davies 1939, 136:182–87).

The two words that Paul used in 1 Corinthians 2:1 are the same he used throughout the first chapter, *logos* and *sophia*, "word" and "wisdom." Of course, *logos* also means "intelligence," as well as the expression of that intelligence. It is the means of expressing that which is in your mind. "Speech" would be a good rendering. Paul is saying here that there is no superiority in speech.

This calls to mind an experience of Vincent Ferrier, an eloquent preacher of the 15th century, when called to preach before a high dignitary of state. He took care to prepare his sermon according to the rules of oratory, but it was a signal failure. Next day he preached in his usual style, without pretentiousness, and electrified his hearers. The dignitary, who had heard him on both occasions, asked him how he could account for so great a difference in his sermons. He answered, "Yesterday Vincent Ferrier preached; today Jesus Christ."

The second word, *sophia,* is natural wisdom, used here again as the means of proclaiming the truth of the gospel. Since Paul all along has argued that natural wisdom can never lead a person to faith in Christ, why give it any superiority over the very content of the gospel? This also means that we should not in any way try to conform the gospel to human wisdom. Natural wisdom must never be made the judge of God's actions. Your mind and mine must never question God.

That this is Paul's intent is further shown by the choice of the participle *katangellōn,* "declaring or preaching." This compound verb is made up of the preposition *kata,* "down," and *angellō,* "to announce." It is as if you were standing on a height to announce something to those below. It has the meaning of an authoritative proclamation that you had better deliver unadulterated and that those who hear it had better accept without question. This verb is used six times by Paul (Rom. 1:8, 1 Cor. 2:1; 9:14; 11:26, Phil. 1:16, 18, Col. 1:28) and ten times in Acts (4:2; 13:5, 38; 15:36; 16:17, 21; 17:3, 13, 23; 26:23). It is declaring a fact.

And what was it that Paul was so categorically proclaiming to the Corinthians? The Authorized Version calls it "the testimony of God," but several other manuscripts render it "the mystery of God." In Greek that would be *mustērion* instead of *marturion.* The word *marturion,* "testimony," occurs in 1 Corinthians 1:6 as the testimony that has God as its source. This is all that God did and proclaimed. Paul recognizes his prophetic responsibility to transmit facts faithfully, uncolored or unchanged by human words or wisdom. If we accept those manuscripts that use the word "mystery," then it would include the message from God, but it would further add the element that what God did and said is a mystery, is inexplicable by human words and wisdom. We can proclaim it, but we can hardly explain it. It is real, but it eludes human scrutiny. Therefore it has to be proclaimed with authority and is not to be tampered with.

Is this concept of God's message, of all He said and did as "mystery," a cause for discouragement? I do not think so. On the contrary, it inspires us to greater effort in the study of His Word, to discover all that may be known of Him, and it keeps us looking forward to that day when we shall see Him face to face, and know even as we are known.

> Admit a God—that mystery supreme!
> That cause uncaused! All other wonders cease:
> Nothing is marvelous for Him to do;
> Deny Him—all is mystery besides.

LESSONS:

1. A pastor's first concern should be the salvation of his people.

2. Paul was not only an extremely intelligent and capable man, but he also used his mind to its fullest, God-given potentiality.

3. Paul declares that speech and wisdom are not superior to the content of the gospel.

4. We are all to use our abilities fully, but with humility, recognizing that they are God-given.

1 Cor. 2:2 | *Human Reason and the Gospel*

For I determined not to know anything among you, save Jesus Christ, and him crucified.

Using Head and Heart in Preaching the Gospel

How many aimless people there are in the world! They awake in the morning without a plan; they make no program. Every man needs a goal in life. It gives definiteness to all his processes of thought and action. Life is not a question of separate actions. It is a central purpose.

The apostle Paul had such a goal. His purpose in life was to lead men and women to the Savior. He knew that all men are sinners—lost and in need of salvation (1 Cor. 1:18, Rom. 3:23). For people to become rich in material things or in thought is not enough. No amount of wealth or knowledge can save a soul or help men get rid of the sense of guilt that tortures them.

Paul could not hide the supreme purpose of his life, nor did he try to. "God forbid that I should glory, save in the cross of our Lord Jesus Christ," he said. "I am not ashamed of the gospel of Christ: for it is the power of God unto salvation to every one that believeth. . . . Neither count I my life dear unto myself, so that I might finish my course with joy, and the ministry, which I have received of the Lord Jesus. . . . I am ready not to be bound only, but also to die at Jerusalem for the name of the Lord Jesus." (Gal. 6:14, Rom. 1:16, Acts 20:24; 21:13; Parker 1959, 26: 202–9).

When Paul came to Corinth, he came for no other purpose than to preach the gospel and to see sinful hearts cleansed by the power of the blood of Christ. That was his goal. That is what he calls the witness of God, or the mystery that belongs to God. It has its beginning, its source with God, and us humans as its object.

In verse 2, he amplifies what he said in verse 1, that he had not come to them with any superiority of word or wisdom. He was fully equipped to come in such a manner, of course. But he knew that no words or human argumentation would suffice to reach the goal of converting sinners. "Therefore," he says, "I did not judge it proper to know among you anything but Jesus Christ and him crucified." "What a narrow-minded bigot!" many people would say. But let us not be hasty in our estimate of Paul and his apostolic policy.

We must first look into what is implied by the principal verb he uses here. It is *ekrina*, the first aorist of the Greek verb *krinō*. It is unfortunate that the Authorized Version translates this word "determined," for determination may be mistaken as more the result of man's will than as involving primarily—though not exclusively—the exercise of his mind. A determined person may want to do something in spite of what his better judgment dictates.

The word *krinō* is related in root to the Latin *cerno*, which means "to sunder, that is, to part, to sift." It is to divide out, to select, to make an evaluation, to decide, to judge, to assess. That is what a judge does, and that is why he is called *kritēs* in Greek, from the same verb. His duty is to measure the evidence without involving his will and personality, to decide whether a person is guilty or not.

The judgment in Greek is called *krisis* (Matt. 5:21, 22; 10:15, 2 Pet. 2:4). Paul therefore says, "I made a judgment, I examined all the circumstances, I evaluated them, and I made a decision." This of course was always in view of the central goal of his life and his coming to Corinth—the conversion of sinners. As a judge must constantly have before him the law and its requirements, so Paul had before him the need of the Corinthians and the Savior who could satisfy that need.

Paul was a thinker, for judgment in any situation requires thought. In 1 Corinthians 2:1 he in no way negates the value of personal judgment and decision, but rather affirms the necessity of them. He was not like that preacher whose sermons were neither attractive nor effective, and who prayed in his morning service that he might have power. A member of the congregation shouted out, "It is ideas you want, sir, not power." There is real truth in that criticism. We are so prone to be one-sided in our approach to human needs. Some use only ideas, some use only power—as if God is divorced from the mind and there is only heart. Our personalities consist of both, and God is the author of both.

It is childish to think that Paul in this passage was actually repudiating the method of his preaching among the people in the previous cities that he had visited in Greece: Philippi, Thessalonica, Berea, and Athens. His preaching in all places was both in divine wisdom and in divine power. *Ekrina,* he says in 1 Corinthians 2:2—I made a judgment in view of what I was trying to accomplish and of the need of the people to whom I came.

Nor did Paul mean that a man in the pulpit should not clothe the gospel of Jesus Christ in the very best words possible. Words or human wisdom, as Paul stressed in verse 1, should not have superiority over the fact of Christ and Him crucified. Nor should words in any way obscure the fact. Words are like the pipe that carries the water to a thirsty soul. The water is the important thing, for it alone can quench human thirst. But the pipe should be of good quality and clean if the water is to reach us in its purest state. Let us not despise either the one or the other, but give each its rightful place.

A tight-fisted Christian, annoyed by the appeals of his preacher for funds, burst out one day, "Pastor, does not the Bible declare that the water of life is free, that grace is without money?" "Yes," replied the preacher, "but it takes pipes to channel the water to the people, and pipes cost money."

We must judge the apostle not only by his words, which may sometimes be misunderstood, but by his example, which is clearer than words. We find that in preaching there was no one more eloquent than Paul; and in his writing eloquence is evident in every epistle that came from his pen. In this he was not departing from the principle established by his Lord. In spite of the depth of the Lord's teaching, which even the wisest could not fully plumb, there was an attraction for all. The common people heard him gladly. Our Lord presented the mystery of God with a wisdom of thought, with a wealth of imagination, and an excellency of speech, which have ever since been unrivaled, unique. The clothing of the gospel in fitting language is required by God who gave us mind, and who gave us speech (Georgeson 1907, 71:194, 195).

The Uses and Limitations of Human Reason

The apostle Paul was a man of judgment. In 1 Corinthians 2:1 he told the Corinthian church, I did not come to you with superiority of words or wisdom, because I made my judgment that this course was necessary in your case and for what I was trying to accomplish. *Ekrina*, "I judged or decided," is in the aorist indicative, which here means that it was a definite judgment made at a definite time for a specific reason. Paul by no means despised wisdom or philosophy as such. If this were his meaning, then it would be wrong for Christians to study philosophy or speech. Yet these are departments of importance, not only in our secular institutions of higher learning, but also in Christian colleges and universities. There is much evidence to indicate that Paul was familiar with the philosophers and secular writers of his day. Speaking to the Athenians, you remember, he referred to their secular poets (Acts 17:28).

There are secular realms of life in which we must participate, and from which we cannot divorce ourselves. Though we are not of the world, we are still in the world and must be aware of much that is to be learned from it. If we did not know these indispensable secular truths we could not make sound judgments. But the difference between a non-Christian and a Christian in this respect is the ability to know and to judge what each element in life can accomplish.

Neither philosophy nor natural science can eliminate the sense of guilt resulting from man's sinful nature. Recognize that basic fact and you stand a chance of looking for your redemption in areas other than your own or the natural world. Many things can be discovered by the proper use of reason. But there are also many that cannot. If you recognize the first, you are humanly wise, if the second as well, you are wise according to God. But he who is possessed of divine wisdom need not be devoid of natural wisdom, for the latter is useful in its own realm of the mundane, the earthly. One of the greatest discoveries you can make is that, although reason may be admirable and the uses of it noble in the lower order, there are certain realms of truth, there are certain sorts of knowledge, for which reason is not adapted.

It will help us to know what Paul meant by the declaration, "Therefore I decided not to know anything among you, but Jesus Christ and him crucified," if we exclude first of all what he did not mean. He did not mean that in going to Corinth he was not going to talk about or listen to anything else except the crucified Christ. As a human being he would naturally speak about the weather, about health, food, business, nature, human relationships, man's duty to his government, and similar matters. Misunderstanding of a verse like this has led some Christians to make themselves obnoxious to others, by narrowing their conversation to nothing else but the Lord Jesus Christ and Him crucified. Such people are more likely to repel others than to lead them to a saving knowledge of Christ.

The man who charges up to a perfect stranger to demand, "Are you saved?" may indeed be zealous for the Lord, but he shows very little understanding or love for his fellowman. His tactless approach indicates that he has no real interest in the man as a person, but only as a potential candidate for conversion, an object for witnessing to. Common sense is essential even in witnessing. Remember this. You should witness not for the sake of witnessing but for the purpose of winning souls to Christ. As a fisher of men you must exercise judgment in casting the net. Or, to change the simile, you must hold your fire until you see the target. Firing your rifle into the air will not accomplish anything. Let this be the judgment you exercise as a steward of the higher truths of life.

Paul is not a mere thoughtless fanatic. Observe the infinitive he uses in this verse when he says he is determined not "to know" anything among them but Jesus Christ and Him crucified. It is *eidenai*, from *oida*, meaning "to know by reflection," in contradistinction to *gignōskō*, "to know by experience." It is a principle of thought that Paul expresses here. He fully knew by experience. He realized that the Corinthians and all human beings had and have many needs besides the forgiveness of their sins through the blood of Christ. And he discusses these many needs in his two epistles to them. He presents Christ crucified, not as the One who would exclude the consideration of all other things that pertain to life, but as the one ingredient that animates everything, makes everything worthwhile. In Jesus Christ, he asserts, he found an all-sufficient comprehensiveness, and they could, too. It is not Jesus Christ and nothing else, but it is Jesus Christ in everything.

Life cannot be departmentalized. It is absurd for a segment of the American public to think that God and Jesus Christ must be separated from our educational processes. Education is absolutely necessary, Paul declares, but it is essentially deficient without Christ crucified. What is the use of learning in a psychology class of the various guilt complexes without learning where you can lose them—at the foot of Calvary's cross?

As Alexander Maclaren says, what Paul meant to say is not that he excluded anything but that he found "everything in" Christ. You cannot derive the fullest satisfaction from foods, health, love, education, entertainment, travel, or anything else, if Christ is missing from it. "I have decided," Paul declares in effect, "that no matter what I discuss it will never be without the basic consideration of Christ and Him crucified."

Thus, when I as a Christian husband look upon a woman, I may admire her, but the image of my wife in the sacredness of marriage is constantly before me. I look upon food as a means to strengthen me to please Christ. He becomes central in my life. He is included in everything, for He is life. What do you lack when you become a Christian and receive Jesus Christ as your Savior? Absolutely nothing. You add Christ to everything, and everything then takes on a meaning and a glory it never had before. That is exactly what Christ promised in Matthew 6:33: "But seek ye first the kingdom of God, and his righteousness; and all these things shall be added unto you." In Christ you never lose but always gain, if He is first and in all things.

A Unique Salvation Through a Unique Savior

Paul, like a good parent, keenly felt his responsibility toward those whom he had led to Christ in Corinth. They were his children in the Lord, whose faltering steps must be guided into right paths of belief and conduct.

As Maclaren, elaborates:

> Paul felt that, if he was to give the Corinthians what they needed, he must refuse to give them what they wanted, and whilst he crossed their wishes he was consulting their necessities. . . . In the message of Christ and Him crucified, there lies in germ the satisfaction of all that is legitimate in these desires that at first sight it seems to thwart. Paul determined to know nothing but Jesus, and to know everything in Jesus, and Jesus in everything. Do not begin your building at the second floor windows. Put in your foundations first, and be sure that they are well laid. Let the sacrifice of Christ, in its application to the individual and his sins, be ever the basis of all that you say. And then, when that foundation is laid, exhibit to your heart's content the application of Christianity and its social aspects. But be sure that the beginning of them all is the work of Christ for the individual sinful soul, and the acceptance of that work by personal faith [Maclaren 1903, 273–86].

Paul recognized an exclusive central position to the cross of Jesus Christ: "To know nothing but Jesus Christ, and him crucified." He himself preached Christ, but he could not take the place of, or do the work of Christ. He knew that the Corinthians sought to exalt the preacher instead of the One preached. Thus they claimed to be of Apollo, of Peter, or of Paul. No, he said, I do not recognize any human being capable of being or doing what Christ did. The preacher must efface himself, like a man in a gallery displaying masterpieces to the eyes of the beholders. He must never seek to project himself when he preaches, but only Christ and the message of the cross.

Remember what John the Baptist answered when he was asked, "Who art thou?" "I am a voice," he said. He was like that great artist who wore a lamp on his cap to prevent his shadow from being thrown upon the picture he was painting. How much more careful we should be lest the shadow of self fall on those to whom we preach the gospel.

Paul told us in the first chapter of 1 Corinthians that the Jews required a sign . . . but "We preach Christ crucified." The Greeks sought after wisdom . . . but again, "We preach Christ crucified." These two demands are representative, in an emphatic way, of two sets of desires and mental characteristics that divide the world between them.

On the one hand, there is the sensuous tendency that wants something done for it, something to see, something that sense can grasp at, and so, as it fancies, lifts itself upwards into a higher region. "The Jew requires a sign"—that is, not merely a miracle, but something to look at. He wants a visible sacrifice; he wants a priest. He wants religion largely to consist in the doing of certain acts that may be supposed to bring, in some magical fashion, spiritual blessings.

And Paul, in oppositon to that says, "We preach Christ crucified." We are so likely in our Christian worship to drift toward the more ornate rituals and aesthetic services, as a means of attracting people to church, considering them more important than proclaiming Christ. We should be careful lest we substitute the shadow for the substance. The Christ of the cross demands an exclusive place in our worship and preaching. We must never conform to the desires of men by substituting for the simple glory of the preached Word the attractions of a sensuous worship.

Further, "The Greeks seek after wisdom." They wanted demonstration, abstract principle, systematized philosophies, and the like. Paul comes again with his "We preach Christ, and him crucified." In this day and age, we are expected to preach precepts of morality and social justice instead of the gospel of the crucified Christ. For the most part the pulpit has turned into a Sunday supplement to the daily newspaper. And then we wonder why people stay home to read their papers. It is because in church they fail to hear of Christ and Him crucified (*Ibid.,* 279–82).

Is it enough to recognize the Lord Jesus and preach Him apart from His substitutionary atonement? Paul did not believe so. His determination was to know "Jesus Christ, and him crucified." Why did Paul add that last phrase? He knew that to dilate on Christ's character and teachings and lovely deeds would not effect the salvation of the Corinthians. With all their art and culture and affluence, their society was abominably corrupt. Only Christ "as having been crucified" could accomplish such a miracle. Paul refers to a fact of history in this phrase. Yet it is not the mere recognition that Christ was crucified that is important, but the person of the Lord Jesus Christ and what He accomplished for us on the cross.

Three fundamental facts must be believed for any sinner to find salvation: the Lord Jesus Christ's humanity, His deity, and His substitutionary atonement on the cross. Paul declared that this Man whom he determined to preach among the Corinthians was "Jesus." That was His human name, which means Savior. "And she shall bring forth a son, and thou shalt call his name Jesus: for he shall save his people from their sins" (Matt. 1:21).

Interestingly, the personal pronoun "he" in this verse is designated by the emphatic demonstrative pronoun *autos,* implying that only He can do this. The "he" in Greek could have been indicated by a simple suffix if no emphasis and singularity were meant. We have another demonstrative pronoun, in the third person singular, *touton,* in 1 Corinthians 2:2, in the phrase "and him crucified," literally, "and this one crucified."

In order for this person to be able to save, He must be recognized as Jesus, a fully human being, and yet without sin. He was born of a woman (Gal. 4:4). He who became the bridge, the Mediator between a Holy God and sinful man, is called "the man Christ Jesus" (1 Tim. 2:5). It is just as much heresy to reject His humanity as it is to reject His deity. If He were not man, He could not have suffered physical death.

Paul preached Jesus the Man who was crucified. But he also speaks of Him as Christ. That is His divine name, the Anointed One from the foundation of the world. He was the promised Messiah. He was God who became man in order to die as the God-Man. In this He was unique; and His accomplishment for man—his salvation—is also unique.

What Can Save the World?

Leonardo da Vinci once took a friend of his to see his masterpiece of the "Last Supper." The friend's initial comment was, "The most striking thing in the picture is the cup." The artist immediately took his brush and wiped out the cup, saying, "Nothing in my painting shall attract more attention than the face of my Master."

The apostle Paul was equally single-minded in his devotion to his Lord. The center of his theology was Jesus Christ and the blood that He shed for our sakes on the cross. Whether men like it or not, whether they consider it foolishness or not, it is the only remedy for their sinfulness.

You recall the account of certain Greeks in Jerusalem who came to Philip one day, saying they wanted to see Jesus. Philip came and told Andrew, and together they told the Lord. Have you ever wondered at the answer the Lord gave them? He did not say, "Bring them along; I will be glad to have your Greek friends see Me." With an abruptness that, if not understood, is surprising He said, "The hour is come that the Son of man should be glorified." And how was this to be accomplished? "Except a grain of wheat fall into the ground and die, it abideth alone: but if it die, it bringeth forth much fruit" John 12:20–24).

It is by the process of dying that the wheat multiplies, and it is by the process of Christ's dying that Christ multiplies, in the lives of those who accept His sacrifice by faith. You cannot become a Christian merely by trying to imitate the life and example of Christ. This is an impossibility while you are still clothed in your sinfulness. You can only be saved by the death of Jesus.

Again I ask, is Paul narrow-minded in his determination to preach Christ crucified and nothing else? Think a bit. Is acceptance of the atoning work of Christ the answer to all of mankind's ills? How about our social and political and personal problems? If people were saved from sin and loved a life of personal righteousness, seeking God's will instead of their own, every public problem would be on the way to being solved.

You would settle the divorce problem, for instance. The other day I came across this piece of news:

> Adherents to 'That Old Time Religion' [i.e., those whose sins have been washed by the blood of Jesus Christ] are more likely to have happy marriages than their Evangelical, Catholic, and liberal Protestant counterparts [i.e., those who in large part are merely church affiliated but not born again], a University of Southern California research study shows. Quantitatively and qualitatively, Pentecostals [who preach and practice salvation through the blood of Christ] scored highest in marital adjustment of all the Christian groups studied. More of them had happier marriages, according to a doctoral dissertation by Allen G. Snider, who recently earned his Ph.D. in sociology at USC Rankings based on a survey of 208 couples in the Los Angeles area indicate that the Evangelical religions scored second highest, Roman Catholics third, and liberal Protestants lowest in marital adjustment.

It is easier to make marital family adjustments when you are cleansed by the blood of Christ. As a Christian husband, you realize you are to love your wife enough to die for her. And the Christian wife is to love her husband so much that no personal consideration will hinder her from doing her best to please him. You cannot do these things in your sinful state. But once you allow Christ to enthrone Himself within you, you find yourself in a different world.

Or take the relationships between nations. There is an outcry against war from many quarters. But war will be among us as long as we are redeemed. There will be only one period in human history without war, when all shall bow the knee to Christ during the millennium. The absence of war is only possible when the peace of Christ fills every human heart. If everybody loved everybody else enough to die for them, they would not kill them.

"Christ and him crucified" would settle the capital and labor problem in short order. If every employer loved every employee well enough to die for him, and every employee loved every employer in the same way, we would never have another strike.

If everybody accepted and loved "Christ, and him crucified," it would settle the drug and alcohol problem. No one would willingly give his neighbor anything that would harm him in any way. In fact, "Christ, and him crucified," when allowed complete control of our hearts and lives, would settle every problem that perplexes the public mind. He is the solution for politics, economics, statesmanship, and religion. Let our universities crown Him, and learning will have the right relation to everything else in heaven and on earth. Let our businessmen crown Him, and commerce will have the right relation to everything else. Let the home crown Him, and it will be a bit of heaven on earth.

If you as an individual will allow Christ the crucified to cleanse you from sin, you will begin to live a new life in a heavenly world within an earthly one (Dixon n.d., 92–111, and Young 1903, 71–87).

This is not to say that the born-again Christian instantly becomes unselfish and loving toward others overnight. Though we have received a new nature from Christ, the old nature is still within us, and the battle between the two goes on. Only as we allow the crucified Christ to crucify our self-centered desires and motivations will we be able to come into right relationships with others. But as the blood of Christ continually cleanses us from sin, we shall be humbled and willing to seek the highest good of our fellowmen, even as our Lord who came not to be served but to serve.

Some years ago several congressmen, who were devout Christians, were taking a walk one evening. Their conversation drifted to the subject of religion and the state of the world. They were not enthusiastic about the outlook and were just about to agree that the whole world was on the toboggan when they chanced to pass a little chapel. From within came the words of a familiar hymn:

> There is a fountain filled with blood
>   Drawn from Immanuel's veins;
> And sinners plunged beneath that flood,
>   Lose all their guilty stains.

As his face lighted up, one said to the other, "As long as people get together and sing that song, there is hope for the world, after all."

LESSONS:

1. Human needs are not one-sided but involve both the mind and heart, and God is the author of both.

2. Paul believed a man in the pulpit should clothe the gospel of Jesus Christ in the best words possible.

3. Paul presents Christ crucified, not as the One who would exclude the consideration of all other things that pertain to life, but as the one ingredient that animates everything, makes everything worthwhile.

4. Three fundamental facts which must be believed for the sinner to find salvation include: the Lord Jesus Christ's humanity, His deity, and His substitutionary atonement on the cross.

1 Cor. 2:3 | *God's Strength in Your Weakness*

And I was with you in weakness, and in fear, and in much trembling.

When Is Weakness an Asset?

A great speaker, universally esteemed, sat on the platform before a large audience. Knowing who he was and how able he was, one would think that he would not be nervous in the least. Those on the platform with him, however, were surprised to see that he was trembling. And after he had delivered a powerful address for half an hour he was violently shaking. Would you take that for a sign of weakness or strength? Of course, the audience could not realize how much it cost him to make that speech. Frankly, I feel very much as he did every time I preach. My prayer is that I may never take my responsibility so lightly, or consider it so commonplace, that I cease to tremble and fear lest I fail my Lord. Only under the pressure of such urgency can the Christian minister offer anything worthwhile to his listeners.

It is not cowardly to experience such emotions. Heroism is sensitive to danger. Strength is sensitive to weakness. In real courage there is always a realistic element of fear. The apostle Paul, for instance, was one of the greatest, bravest, ablest men who ever lived. He brought the gospel to Europe. He authored

the finest, most valuable letters ever written. He did more to for-
mulate the theology of the Christian Church than any other
man. He was an intrepid adventurer, a staunch-hearted pioneer,
a leader of almost unexampled greatness. Yet in writing to the
Corinthians, among whom he had lived and labored, he wrote,
"I was with you in weakness, and in fear, and in much trembling." Most of those who have done the greatest work in the
world have felt the same, though they may not have expressed
it in so many words.

Here and there a man will say, "I am the master of my fate:
I am the captain of my soul." Such men are like the rich farmer
of Luke 12 who said to his own soul, "Soul, thou hast much
goods laid up for many years; take thine ease, eat, drink, and be
merry" (v. 19). He thought he was the master of his fate, in command of his soul, but he found out otherwise that night as
death struck him down. Man makes his foolish boasts, forget-
ting the time-tested adage that "Man proposes but God dis-
poses." A little displacement of the retina of the eye, a tiny
speck on one of the valves of the heart, a slight pain in the left
side, a sudden feeling of dizziness, and there is an end of all foolish boasting.

All men who are truly wise realize their weakness and their
dependence. But the wisest have found a secret source of strength.
"I was with you in weakness, and in fear, and in much trembling,"
said Paul, "but by the grace of God I am what I am" (1 Cor.
15:10). "I can do all things through Christ which strengtheneth me" (Phil. 4:13).

The thought of how Paul felt as he reviewed his coming to
the Corinthians, and how difficult his task among them was,
ought to cheer us in our own difficulties. A great man like him
must often have been depressed. Do not fear you are less of a
saint when you are conscious of your weakness and trembling.
And you ministers of God, cheer up as you shake in your boots

before and after you preach. Paul, too, was often filled with a sense of unworthiness and incapacity. At times he was overwhelmed with a sense of failure. When we are similarly overwhelmed, let us realize we are in good company. Such feelings are common to all who have striven to attain some lofty ideal. The winning of great strength is nearly always the result of conquering weakness. Nobody was ever yet born great, or a saint. The question has often been asked, "Why were the saints, saints?" And these answers have been suggested:

> Because they were cheerful when it was hard to be cheerful; Patient when it was hard to be patient; Because they pushed on when they wished to stand still; And kept silent when they wished to talk; And were agreeable when they wished to be disagreeable.

Those whom we envy, almost, for their goodness have reached it "in weakness, and in fear, and in much trembling." The gospel is for weak, sinful men, not for those who are "masters of their fate." This is a reminder that most of us greatly need, for we sometimes feel so keenly our own weakness that there is danger of our becoming paralyzed.

A young soldier who was showing signs of panic on the eve of his first battle was chaffed by a veteran. "Why, sonny," he said, "you're shaking with fear. Do not be such a coward." "I'm not a coward," hotly retorted the youth. "If you felt half as scared as I do, you would run away!" He was right. That young man was not a coward because he felt fear, but he would have been a coward if he had allowed it to master him and drive him from his post of duty.

Paul's weakness, fear, and trembling did not paralyze him into a state of inactivity. Instead, it threw him back on reliance in a strength not his own, that of his Lord, and this made him so daring that he went even to most sinful Corinth to proclaim the gospel. We should not succumb to our fears but use them as stepping stones to higher things. Paul's sense of weakness prodded him into activity instead of paralyzing him. In writing to the Corinthians he enumerates what resulted from his weakness in action:

> In journeying often, in perils of waters, in perils of robbers, in perils by mine own countrymen, in perils by the heathen, in perils in the city, in perils in the wilderness, in perils in the sea, in perils among false brethren; in weariness and painfulness, in watchings often, in hunger and thirst, in fastings often, in cold and nakedness [2 Cor. 11:26, 27].

He would certainly agree with Martin Luther who wrote:

> A mighty fortress is our God,
> A bulwark never failing;
> Our Helper, He, amid the flood
> Of mortal ills prevailing.
> Did we in our own strength confide,
> Our striving would be losing;
> Were not the right man on our side,
> The Man of God's own choosing.
> Doth ask who that may be?
> Christ Jesus, it is He. . . .
> And He must win the battle.

God's Strength in Your Weakness

"When I am weak, then am I strong," said the apostle Paul in 2 Corinthians 12:10. What did he mean by such a seemingly contradictory statement? Well, I can think of at least three good things that a sense of weakness does for us.

First, it keeps us humble and makes us sympathetic. We will not be tempted to boast that we accomplished anything by our unaided efforts—without the help of God and others. There is some truth to the statement that brilliant students rarely make good teachers, because they cannot appreciate the difficulties that the less gifted encounter. But no fair-minded person can despise those who have the same weaknesses he himself has—or once had. If we recognize our own faults we will not be so hard on the faults of others; we will want to help them. Feeling the weight of our own burdens, we will be more inclined to help others bear theirs.

Second, our sense of weakness leads us or drives us to Christ. When all is going well, when we appear to be successful, when we feel we can do what we want to do and are powerful enough to step over the obstacles that lie in our path, we are apt to forget Christ. We act as though we can do without Him, although we would not say that in so many words. But when we are helpless and prostrate, we can only pray. When our own strength is exhausted, we reach out a hand for His.

Third, in reaching out to Christ, our weakness becomes strength—real strength, for it is His, not ours. "I can do all things through Christ which strengtheneth me" (Phil. 4:13; Leyland 1931, 119:78).

Naturally what Paul had in mind when he confessed to weakness, fear, and trembling was his relationship as a preacher of the gospel to sinful men. In the previous verse of this chapter that is made clear. He came preaching the gospel of the crucified Christ. Now what man can actually enforce the results he desires from his preaching of the gospel? Paul's desire was that sinful, lost men and women might be saved. But no man is strong enough to save sinners. Before the obstinacy of sinful men we must recognize our weakness and our inability to bring about the desired goal of their salvation.

That is what every preacher, every witness of the gospel, has to realize. Even omnipotence incarnate in the person of the Lord Jesus Christ wept over unrepentant Jerusalem. "And when he was come near, he beheld the city, and wept over it, saying, If thou hadst known, even thou, at least in this thy day, the things which belong unto thy peace, but now they are hid from thine eyes" (Luke 19:41, 42).

Have you not ever felt like that as you tried to speak to a wayward child, to a sinful husband, wife, father, or mother, and found yourself unable to make them see their need of salvation in Christ? Have you not felt powerless to convince them of the wonderful change that would come into their lives if they would only receive Christ and Him crucified to cleanse them from sin and to give them the power of a victorious life full of peace? What could Paul boast of as he thought of how he desired to see so many more saved than were actually won by his preaching?

When you try to preach the gospel, to do God service, you begin to realize how miserably weak you are, how little you can do, how helpless are all your efforts; and you think that you may as well give up altogether. But Paul did not give up. He believed that where sin abounded, as it did in Corinth, grace could much more abound (Rom. 5:20).

First Corinthians 2:3 begins exactly as does the first verse in this chapter, with the Greek compound word *kagō*. This is made up of *kai*, meaning "and, also," and *egō*, meaning "I." "And I having come to you, brethren," says verse 1. "And I in weakness, and in fear, and in much trembling came unto you," says verse 3.

There are three interrelationships suggested here. There is Paul, there is Jesus Christ and Him crucified, and there are the Corinthians. Paul is endeavoring to clarify his relationship with both the crucified Christ and the Corinthians. No doubt the latter recognized that Paul had faithfully preached the gospel among them. Souls had been saved. But Paul wanted to make it very clear that this was not due to any power resident in himself but to the gospel, which is the power of God unto salvation to everyone who believes. That is why he says "and I" twice in verses 1 and 3. He did not intend to compare himself with other preachers, as some so often like to do.

How you and I stand in contrast with other preachers should never concern us. That is not what will count in the final analysis, but rather how we felt every time we stood up to declare the gospel to others. Has it been in the confidence of the flesh, or in weakness, fear, and trembling? We must never be so pharisaical as to compare our greatness and our goodness with the smallness and misery of others. At best, none of us are really all that God expects us to be.

If it were you and I writing back to a congregation we had established, I wonder what we would have said? Might not our epistle have run something like this. "Was it not great to see so many people responding to my preaching? I am so glad I led so and so to Christ. I am going to head up a clinic on how to be a successful preacher. It is high time other preachers followed my example." Maybe we would not have expressed it quite that obviously, but perhaps we would have felt that way in our hearts. But Paul said nothing of the kind. "And I came unto you in weakness, and in fear, and in much trembling," he declared.

In front of the great Cathedral of Amiens stands a statue of Jesus Christ, and on either side His twelve apostles. Below them are written their greatest virtues, in contrast to their greatest vices. In Peter's case, his outstanding quality is his courage, but below it you see a figure of Peter flying from a leopard, representing his cowardice. Then beneath that you see the same figure sitting on a leopard and riding forth to conquest. The lesson the sculptor wished to teach is that by contact with the Lord Jesus Christ that very thing which is a man's weakness can be transfigured into his strength; that very thing from which he fled becomes the glorious chariot on which he rides forward to conquer.

Preacher, Humble Yourself

Christian witnessing must always be done in a spirit of humility. We have the testimony of the apostle Paul himself for this. The Greek verb used in 1 Corinthians 2:3, translated "I was" in our English Bible, is *egenomēn*, the first person singular of the second aorist of the verb *ginomai*, which means "to become." In verse 1 the verb (used twice) is *elthōn* (participial form, "having come") and *ēkhon*, "I came." But here it is *egenomēn pros humas*, "I became unto you."

Egenomēn, which is from *ginomai*, a deponent verb, is in the indicative middle voice as to its form, but is more active in its meaning, which indicates what Paul turned out to be toward the Corinthians. "I became toward you" and not "with" as the preposition *meta* would have indicated. In this context God's responsibility for the way Paul felt as he came to minister to the Corinthians is not emphasized, but rather Paul's responsible reaction to God's grace and the magnitude of the ministry that God has entrusted to him. "I became on my own," says Paul in effect. "That was a state of being I arrived at." The humbling and the feeling of unworthiness that are necessary to an effective witness for Christ should be intrinsic to our own reaction to the formidable task. We should logically and voluntarily humble ourselves as we undertake the task of proclaiming the gospel. When the subject to be proclaimed is Jesus Christ and Him crucified, and it is to be preached to sinners such as the Corinthians, then the state in which we must place ourselves is that of weakness, fear, trembling.

"Toward" you, not "with" you. There is a difference between the two expressions. "With" the Corinthians Paul was indeed a mighty man of God, an apostle in every sense of the word. He said to them in 2 Corinthians 11:5, 6, "I suppose I was not a whit behind the very chiefest apostles . . . but we have been thoroughly made manifest among you in all things." The Lord spoke to Paul while he was undergoing persecution in Corinth, saying, "Be not afraid, but speak, and hold not thy peace: for I am with thee, and no man shall set on thee to hurt thee: for I have much people in this city" (Acts 18:9, 10). God gave Paul courage, and He commanded him not to be afraid while he was with the Corinthians who sought to put him in jail.

But when it came to how Paul felt as he preached the gospel to sinners, he declared he was so weak, so afraid, that he trembled. This was not because he doubted the power of the gospel, but because he knew that of himself he could do nothing to cause men to respond to it. He knew how difficult these Corinthians were to persuade of their need of a Savior. He knew he could not convert them on his own. He knew that the natural inclination of a sinner is to resist the gospel. He realized that even for the most eloquent, the most capable preacher—even for a great apostle as himself—the most difficult thing on earth is to convert a sinner to Christ.

This requires a power far greater than any human being possesses. When we seek to win others to Christ, we must never think we possess such power, or lead others to believe we do through any air of superiority or lightness as we proclaim the gospel. We would do well to heed the advice of Dr. Payson, who said, "Paint Jesus Christ upon your canvas, and then hold Him up to the people, but so hold Him up that not even your little finger can be seen."

"I became weak, fearful, and trembling toward you," said Paul. Not "I gave the appearance of being that way," but "that is the way I really felt and was." This was no hypocritical pretension, but a real state of being. Are you truly conscious of your inadequacies as you face the sinner with the gospel of Jesus Christ, or is your humility a mere pretense? How we need to beware of hypocrisy, lest we secretly believe ourselves to be strong and great but put on a show of humility toward others. God can detect whether you are truly conscious of your weakness, and only then will His strength be manifested in and through you

The word translated "weakness" is *astheneia* in Greek. It is made up of the privative *a*, "without," and the noun *sthenos*, "strength." "Without strength" is the literal meaning. To be weak is to stumble. This word refers basically though not exclusively to physical weakness or sickness. When our Lord spoke of Lazarus' ailment, He said, "This sickness [*astheneia*] is not unto death" (John 11:4). In the New Testament, *astheneia* (sickness, weakness) and the adjectival noun *asthenēs* (sick, weak) "are hardly ever used of purely physical weakness, but frequently in the comprehensive sense of the whole man, e.g., the 'weaker sex' in 1 Peter 3:7" (Kittel 1964, 1:491).

I believe Paul is referring not so much to sickness or weakness of body as to weakness in general. The same word is used in 1 Corinthians 1:27: "And the weak [*asthenē*] things of the world God chose that he may put to shame the strong things." Weakness stands in contrast to strength. It is therefore the general state of weakness that Paul refers to. True, he was physically weak, as we gather from 2 Corinthians 12:7, where he speaks of his "thorn in the flesh." But the expression *egenomēn pros humas* (I became toward you) denotes rather an attitude than a permanent state of being. "I became weak," I took upon myself that attitude that if your salvation were to be effected it would not be accomplished through any power that I possessed, either of body or mind.

Furthermore, the preposition *en* meaning "in," which introduces these three attitudes—weakness, fear, and trembling—and is also used in verse 4 in the expression "not in enticing words of man's wisdom, but in [*en*] demonstration of the Spirit and of power," indicates an attitude, not a physical state. (Note that the correct translation is "in" in verse 4, not "with," as the Authorized Version has it.)

There is no doubt that Paul suffered from some bodily infirmity—just what is not clear—to which reference is made in 1 Corinthians 12:7. But I do not believe he was referring to his "thorn in the flesh" when he wrote in 1 Corinthians 2:3 that when he came to Corinth he became weak, that is that he was physically ill. He came with the consciousness of his own personal inadequacy to make the preaching of the gospel effective in the lives of sinners. That is the consciousness that every one of us should have as we proclaim the gospel. That is how John Very felt when he wrote: "I would not speak Thy Word, but by Thee stand while Thou dost to thine erring children speak; O help me but to keep Thine own command, and in my strength to feel me ever weak."

The Folly of Self-Confidence

Did you ever stop to think that recognizing your own weakness and inadequacy was a first and necessary step to your becoming strong? It is no proof of your spiritual advancement that you feel capable of doing anything for God. "Because thou sayest, I am rich, and increased with goods, and have need of nothing"—how does it continue?—"and knowest not that thou art wretched, and miserable, and poor, and blind, and naked: . . ." Thus Christ rebuked the Laodicean church in Revelation 3:17.

If we feel strong of ourselves, we are apt to look to ourselves, and to think that we can manage very well on our own. We feel that we can overcome our enemies and gain for ourselves and for others a passage to the kingdom of heaven. But when we feel weak, we are more disposed to go to Him who alone can give all strength, to Him who is all strength, our Lord Jesus Christ.

As Psalm 75:3 says, "The earth and all the inhabitants thereof are weak [dissolved]: I bear up the pillars of it." Every day of our lives we have some duty to perform for God that we are likely to shrink from. Our sense of inadequacy whispers to us, "You cannot do it." Yet the same apostle who confessed his own weakness and fears said, "I can do all things through Christ which strengtheneth me" (Phil. 4:13).

If we have any real difficulty, there is no kind of help, no kind of strength, no kind of comfort that we need that God is not ready to give us. He not only has the right help, but it comes exactly at the right moment, and in the right way. Only notice this: as it is never a moment too late, so it is rarely a moment too soon. When the children of Israel were about to cross the Jordan, Joshua commanded the priests to take up the ark and go down into the river. "Into the river!" they might have said. "But it is impossible. We shall be swept away. We cannot cross. Let God work such a miracle as He did at the Red Sea. Let Him bid the waters to part hither and thither, and we will trust in Him and go down at once."

Yes, but that was exactly what God was not about to do. He commanded them to go down as it was—the great river before them, foaming and rushing along—and to trust in Him. They obeyed. They came nearer and nearer to the water. Still no sign that God's arm would be stretched out. They reached its very edge, no sign yet. They put their feet into the river. And then, in a moment, in the twinkling of an eye, the waters were stayed on the one side, and stood up in a heap; and on the other they rolled away and left the whole bed of the river dry. Just when the priests felt they were most helpless, just when they saw that they were in the greatest danger, then God stretched out His hand to save them. When they were weak, then they were strong. Or, if you like it in the words of a proverb, "When thou fearest, God is nearest."

The source of triumphant living is not the strong will that refuses to bend or budge, but the will that yields itself to higher power. Only when the Christian senses a feeling of weakness creeping over him and realizes that, in his strength alone, he is inadequate for the task, does he possess true conquering power.

One of the best hours of his life is when, through sickness, toil, or persecution, he feels his physical powers giving way, and his soul rises to claim the occasion for God and his humanity. Knowing that while he himself is weak, the needed power is within easy reach, he is strong. In such a crisis, to become self-confident is to be like the hunted partridge which, seeking escape, confidently enters the trap set for its destruction. Strength comes when, overwhelmed with a sense of unutterable weakness, one flings himself at the feet of Christ and prays as did the sinking disciple, "Lord, save me!"

Our weakness attracts God's attention. A mother responds in exactly the same way. She loves all her children, but if she has one who is weak and delicate, while the others are healthy and strong, her care and attention are lavished upon the one who has most need of her protection, most claim upon her love. Her other children are well able to take care of themselves, but the little delicate one, whose life hangs almost by a thread, appeals by his very weakness to her strongest instincts of maternal love. So it is with our gracious Savior. He loves us, oh, so tenderly, because of our very weakness.

How true this is in our times of severe temptation! No man ever sought refuge from temptation in self-confidence who, in the strain of battle, did not find his fortress crumbling into dust, while he himself suffered humiliating defeat. Simon Peter learned this truth. Strong and boastful in his self-assertiveness, he stood amid the gathering shadows of the world's darkest and most tragic night and smiled as one who gladly greets the dawning of his wedding day. He was confident beyond question that he was equal to any emergency that might arise. It was easy for him to boast and to proclaim loudly what he would do.

Beholding the same fast-deepening shadows, Christ fell to His knees in prayer, and with broken voice and heavy, blood-stained sweat, pleaded for His Father to remove this cup of suffering. Christ, the everlasting Conqueror, prayed for escape from trial, while Peter filled with self-assurance, bade the coming of the worst with defiant spirit, saying, "Though I should die with thee, yet will I not deny thee" (Matt. 26:35).

What a marked contrast between the way these two met the same struggle! But the whole world knows the outcome. In the presence of trial, Peter's strength was scattered like a heap of dry leaves. When he was strong in his estimation, then he was weak. Christ, on the contrary, without His cup of sacrifice being taken away, walked forth strong enough to win a world from sin, while Peter sank in shame. But when, a few hours later, we find the defeated disciple all alone in midnight darkness, weeping like a little child over his weakness, we rejoice, for we know now that Pentecost has found its preacher and the world has found a mighty champion for God.

How to Meet Temptation, Sorrow, and Sin

Temptation is a terrible thing. It is a band of armed robbers, storming the house of the soul, to carry away everything of value. To yield is to have your soul ransacked and burned as though by fire. To face it confidently in your own strength is utter folly. How dangerous it is to listen to those psychologist preachers who urge us to self-confident living. What we need is to realize our weakness and full dependence upon an almighty God. There is only one possibility of victory. In the hour of peril, when eternal destinies depend on your decision, recognize your weakness and fall at the feet of Christ. Cry out with all the earnestness of your frightened soul, "Lord, save me, or I perish." Then victory will fill your heart, and your lips with praise to "him that is able to keep you from falling" (Jude 24).

Apply this same principle of becoming strong in the recognition of your weakness when you face sorrow. Sometimes we feel we should meet sorrow and disappointment with the spirit of a stoic. We clench our fists, and with tight-pressed lips and dry eyes we stand, proud of our strength, defying sorrow to do its worst. We do not want to appear weak before others, so we declare we can bear our own burdens.

But the end of such an attitude is defeat and uncontrolled grief. The burden is so much heavier and the grief so much more bitter than we ever expected that we end up being crushed and overcome. Meanwhile at our side we have seen a frail, weak person whose eyes speak of countless nights of grief and anxiety, but whose serene face and steady voice show us that she has gained the victory over her grief, and in spite of it all has had inner calm and rest. How did this victory come to such a frail person? It came through her own recognition of her frailty. As ripe wheat saves its life by bowing passively before the violent wind, so she bowed low before God at the touch of sorrow. She yielded herself to His will. As Mary and Martha, in their hour of sorrow and bewilderment, forgot everything and fell weeping at the feet of their Lord, so this woman poured out her prayer of utter helplessness to God saying, "Save, Lord, or I perish!" And in her weakness she became strong.

The strength that is needed to meet sorrow comes not from self-control but from tears, not from strength of self but from the consciousness of one's own weakness.

Naturalists are amazed at the resistance of weak things in nature. There is a security and triumph of frail things that baffles man's understanding and imagination. Kay Robinson writes:

> It is a curious thing that the extremes of heat and cold seem to be most easily endured by the flimsiest creatures. What is it that, when the frost is splitting our strongest metal water-pipes, protects the tiny tubes

of life-giving moisture in the almost spectral organism of a gnat? Larger things get frostbitten and perish.

In tropical countries the tiniest insects brave the blistering midday heat which shrivels the largest herbage, and drives men, and birds, and animals gasping under shelter. In India a small blue butterfly flits all day about the parched grass or sits in full blaze of the sun where metal or stone becomes so hot that it burns the hand. What heat-resisting secret resides in the minute body of that little butterfly, scarcely thicker than notepaper? Nature's power of preserving life touches the miraculous.

The same God who made the natural world made the spiritual also. Similarly, then, the saints have the least reason to be afraid when they most feelingly recognize their utter weakness and dependence. We prevail by yielding; we succumb to conquer; like those sea-flowers that continue to bloom amid the surf when the rocks are pounded. In acquiescence and diffidence, in yielding and clinging, we triumph over adversity, as the fern survives geological cataclysms and the butterfly the scorching sun.

In celebrating the Feast of Tabernacles, the Jews are required to make their booths sufficiently frail that the stars may be seen through them: thus through the rents of the body and the dislocations of circumstance are we kept face to face with the claims and hopes of a higher world, and the fragile booth in which we painfully dwell is a safer refuge than the walls of iron and gates of brass of a carnal security [Watkinson 1906, 37, 38].

Paul felt this principle to be supremely true as he came to minister to the Corinthians. We should feel the same way as we undertake to serve men. It is not an easy matter to enter into the domain of another's sinfulness or his grief and sorrow. The task is so tremendous, so difficult, that it can paralyze us with fright. We tremble, little realizing that our sense of weakness can become the source of our strength. Rash boldness and overconfidence are not part of the true Christian's equipment. With such a spirit no one should dare to enter the sacred enclosure of another's grief. It is only when you refuse to trust in human strength or wisdom, but in humility go forward in the name of Christ, that you can work successfully for God.

You may feel called upon to do works of charity, as I am. Let us go forth in weakness. Instead of polished speech upon our lips, let there be tears in our eyes. The hungry soul will know that we understand, and will be glad that we have come. In the hour of someone's sorrow, we may be able to give only a silent handclasp, but he will understand and thank God that He sent us to him. You may be sent to lead some sinful soul to Christ. In weakness your words may fail, leaving you nothing to offer but a look of love. That is enough. The sinner will understand, and through the light of your loving look will find a pathway back to God. Only when we are weak are we strong in the service of Christ (Anderson 1922, 97–102).

A minister preached a sermon one evening and then went home utterly discouraged because he felt that he was a failure in the ministry, though at the same time he was greatly burdened for the lost.

Some time past midnight his doorbell rang, and the leader of his choir, who had been counted a skeptic, came to him saying, "Doctor, I am in agony concerning my soul. Your sermon tonight has convicted me of my sin, and I must have help or I shall die." In a very short time he was rejoicing in Christ.

When asked what it was in the sermon that had impressed him, he said, "It was not so much what you said as the way you said it. I could see by the look in your eye and by the very pathos in your voice that you were longing for men to be saved, and I could not resist your message."

Healthy Fear Versus Sinful Mistrust

The apostle Paul came to the Corinthians not only in an attitude of weakness but also of fear. It is only natural to be fearful when you are weak. Just as feeling your own weakness is a virtue for everyone undertaking the task of evangelism, so is healthy fear. It is one of the most powerful emotions in human experience. As Angelo Patri said, "Education consists in being afraid at the right time." Only a fool has no fear.

A young soldier of evident breeding and culture had one peculiarity. He would never drink alcohol with the others. One day the major asked him to take a message to the express agent in town. "Where shall I find him, sir?" he asked. "Just go into Casey's saloon and sit down. He will show up in the course of the afternoon." The soldier drew back and said, "Beg pardon, sir, but can't I meet him some place else?" "Why, what is the matter with Casey's? Are you afraid to go there?" "Yes, sir, because drink was what made me enlist and leave my family in the first place. I was drunk and did not know what I was doing." "You may go," said the major curtly. "I'll find a more accommodating and less cowardly man."

From then on this soldier carried a reputation for cowardice because he avoided a danger he knew he was too weak to face. However, the opinion of the battery changed one day when he was one of the seven chosen to fire a cannon salute to a visiting general. One bag of powder failed to discharge, and the sergeant ordered it pulled out. As it fell to the ground, the men were horrified to see one corner of it ignited. For a breathless moment no one moved. Then this soldier flung himself upon it and with his bare hands smothered the deadly spark. From then on he was the hero of the company. You may depend upon it; the man who is afraid of doing wrong will be brave enough when occasion calls for it.

The Bible plainly teaches there are two kinds of fear. There is the fear that paralyzes action, the fear that is to be overcome. "The Lord is my light and my salvation; whom shall I fear?" cried the psalmist (Ps. 27:1). And the Lord said, "Fear not" (Matt.

10:28). "Perfect love casteth out fear" (1 John 4:18). The Word of God proclaims a faith that conquers anxiety and fright.

But the same Bible contains another message also. "The fear of the Lord is the beginning of wisdom" (Ps. 111:10). The Lord says, "I will put my fear in their hearts, that they shall not depart from me" (Jer. 32:40). Fear of worse things to come turned the prodigal son back home. Fear can be a salutary turning point in a man's life. A preacher who is afraid of the power of sin and its consequences will preach the gospel with that much more courage. Such healthy fear breaks down our cheap optimism that springs from an excessive estimate of our powers. It breaks down our silly trust in superficial reliances such as our oratory and personality in changing a sinner into a saint.

Men in the public eye, especially on the platform, are sometimes given to bombastic pretensions and pride. Paul's philosophy as he preached was not to feel proud but afraid, lest he prove himself inadequate. Behind almost every great achievement of mankind stands a fear. Medical science stems from the fear of disease. I preach because I fear the end that awaits each sinful and unrepentant soul. Hell creates in me a fear that makes me preach with courage. As Shakespeare said, "Security is mortal's chiefest enemy."

There was enough in Corinth to make even the strongest apostle, the ablest preacher, the sternest moralist like Paul afraid. But is it not true that there is enough anywhere in the world to make us afraid? Unfortunately we often tend to be like children: afraid of what we ought not to fear, and not the least afraid of what we should fear. A child will be afraid of a stuffed wild beast and cry out in terror. The same child will play in a room where there is a most contagious disease and have no sense of danger.

Yes, we are like children. We are afraid of what men can do to us, of what they will say, of what they will think. We are afraid of difficulties that God has promised to remove. We are afraid of dangers through which God has promised to protect us. But we show little fear of Satan and those ungodly men who would tempt us to our ruin. We show little fear of God who is able to destroy both soul and body in hell.

It was in the consciousness of this fear that Paul came to preach the gospel among such sinful people as the Corinthians. It was not the fear of what would happen to him in the way of persecution, but the fear of what would happen to the sinful Corinthians if they were not saved. Such fear will impel you to enter the most sinful ghettos and areas of the world to preach the gospel.

That Paul was not afraid of persecution is evident enough when we read what he himself said of his experiences:

> In labours more abundant, in stripes above measure, in prisons more frequent, in deaths oft. Of the Jews five times received I forty stripes save one. Thrice was I beaten with rods, once was I stoned, thrice I suffered shipwreck, a night and a day I have been in the deep. . . . Most gladly therefore will I rather glory in my infirmities, that the power of Christ may rest upon me. Therefore I take pleasure in infirmities, in reproaches, in necessities, in persecutions, in distresses for Christ's sake: for when I am weak, then am I strong [2 Cor. 11:23–25; 12:9, 10].

This fear then does not mean mistrust or doubt, which would keep the mind in a continual apprehension of falling short of salvation, but a distrust of ourselves from a consciousness of our weakness, and of the obstacles in the way, which produces an anxious solicitude to use all the means necessary to salvation. As the poet Barbara E. Cornet confessed:

I tried myself to bring to pass that which I thought should be;
I felt the Lord would profit by a little help from me.
And so I worried and despaired and vainly laboured on
Until my fairest plans had crashed, my choicest visions gone.
And then I knelt before my Lord, chastened, humbled, still,
Ready to let Him work through me, ready to do His will.
And there it was I found success, for then alone my Lord could bless.

Doing God's Work in the Proper Spirit

The apostle Paul experienced a trembling when he went to Corinth to preach the gospel, as he mentions in 1 Corinthians 2:3. This condition denotes self-abasement in the divine presence, a holy reverence of God, originating in the conviction of his absolute dependence upon Him for that grace that works salvation. Fear and trembling go together. They are the outer manifestations of weakness. Only those who recognize their weakness, fear and tremble. Paul in writing to the Philippians commanded them to work out their own salvation "in fear and trembling" (Phil. 2:12).

Thus fear and trembling are characteristic manifestations of your salvation. It is as if you were carrying a precious jewel in your pocket worth millions of dollars. You would guard it with fear and trembling, would you not? You would seek protection other than what you could provide yourself. You would not fool around where such a responsibility was involved. Such a precious jewel is your salvation, either as you practice it in holy living or as you proclaim it to others as the means of their salvation.

Fear in this verse is a warning against carnal confidence, which, if indulged, would lead to the disuse of the means of salvation. And trembling is an admonition against vain presumption, which would lead to dependence upon self-endeavor for salvation. What is here recommended is assurance without carnal security, and labor without spiritual pride. And this meets the case both of those who undervalue and of those who overvalue human agency in the work of salvation.

In our service for Christ, and especially in our Christian witness, "fear and trembling" should also be expressed by all the humility, care, and diligence that we can possibly use. For fear and trembling here are not opposed to that faith and confidence that we ought to have in God, but to pride, conceit, and confidence in ourselves. This is what Paul warns against in Romans 11:20 when he says, "Be not high-minded; but fear."

Fear and trembling are also opposed to carelessness and indifference about our salvation and the salvation of others—an attitude that is all too common in many of our churches today, not to mention society at large. When Paul admonished the Philippians to work out their own salvation "with fear and trembling," he meant that they should not be careless and secure, but solicitous, diligent, and industrious in it. As "servants must obey their masters with fear and trembling" (Eph. 6:5), and we must all "serve God with reverence and godly fear" (Heb. 12:28), so we must work out our salvation too, lest we fall short of God's will for us by our own default and negligence in looking after it.

In doing God's work, and especially in soul-winning, always remember that we have the power of Almighty God Himself always ready to assist us in it. His grace is always sufficient for us, His strength is made perfect in our weakness. It is He who "worketh in us both to will and to do," and there is no limit to what we may do by Him who can do all things (Beveridge 1824, 2:371–76).

Bishop Latimer once preached a sermon before King Henry VIII that greatly offended his royal auditor by its plainness. The King ordered him to preach again the next Sunday and to make public apology for his offense. The Bishop ascended the pulpit and read his text, and thus began his sermon:

> Hugh Latimer, dost thou know before whom thou art this day to speak? To the high and mighty Monarch, the King's most excellent Majesty, who can take away thy life if thou offendest. Therefore take heed that thou speakest not a word that may displease.
>
> But then, consider well, Hugh! Dost thou not know from whom thou comest—upon whose message thou art sent? Even by the great and mighty God, who is all-present and beholdeth all thy ways, and who is able to cast thy soul into hell! Therefore take care that thou deliverest thy message faithfully.

And so beginning, he preached over again, but with increased energy, the same sermon he had preached the week before. The fear of God delivered him from the fear of man. It is such fear and trembling that Paul demonstrated as he preached to the Corinthians. "And I was with you in weakness, and in fear, and in much trembling" (Neale 1875, 2:249–55, and Hastings 1913, 302).

LESSONS:

1. The winning of great strength is nearly always the result of conquering weakness.

2. Three good things that a sense of weakness does for us include: keeping us humble and making us sympathetic, leading or driving us to Christ, and in reaching out to Christ, becoming real strength, His strength.

3. We should logically and voluntarily humble ourselves as we undertake the task of proclaiming the gospel.

4. Recognizing our own weakness and inadequacy is a first and necessary step to becoming strong, for when we feel weak, we are more disposed to go to Him who alone can give all strength.

5. Rash boldness and overconfidence are not part of the true Christian's equipment. With such a spirit no one should dare to enter the sacred enclosure of another's grief.

6. You may depend upon it; the man who is afraid of doing wrong will be brave enough when occasion calls for it.

7. Fear and trembling go together. They are the outer manifestations of weakness. Only those who recognize their weakness, fear and tremble.

8. Fear and trembling are also opposed to carelessness and indifference about our salvation and the salvation of others.

9. The fear of God delivers us from the fear of man.

1 Cor. 2:4

Prove Your Faith

And my speech and my preaching was not with enticing words of man's wisdom but in demonstration of the Spirit and of power.

How to Witness Effectively for Christ

If God were to call you to enter a great city in order to influence it for Christ, how would you go about it—particularly if it were a city given over to heathen practices and beliefs? You would probably feel the greater the city, the greater your sense of inadequacy.

Such a city was Corinth in the days of the apostle Paul. It was distinguished for its splendor, wealth, pleasure, influence, luxury, and utmost license. It stood second to none in these respects. It was the central point between Greece and Asia on the east, and Rome and Italy and the whole Western world in the other direction. Streams of men actuated by motives of pleasure, or business, or curiosity were constantly passing both ways, tarrying for a time at this central point, making it a truly cosmopolitan center.

Then one day a Christian Jew entered Greek Corinth. His personal appearance lacked distinction. He had sent out no advance advertising party, as do famous evangelists today. He did not even have a local committee to invite him and prepare the way for him. He went uninvited into a strange city, where he was unwanted even by his own countrymen who resided there. They regarded him as a defector from the Jewish faith, though actually he had fulfilled it in Christ. He was completely opposed to the reigning religious sentiment of Corinth, which was polytheistic. He had no financial or other human backing. He was a poor foreigner, a craftsman who made tents for a living. Who would pay any attention to such a man?

We marvel that Paul dared to go to Corinth with the purpose of influencing it for Christ. He put up at the home of a poor man, a tentmaker like himself. And he began to teach doctrines totally at variance with all the religions of Jews and Gentiles. And yet Paul's entrance proved to be the most memorable event that ever occurred in Corinth. Something like this could happen in your case, too, with regard to some sinful community that the Holy Spirit might burden your heart to enter.

When Paul came to Corinth, he knew what his purpose was. He did not come to produce a favorable impression, humanly speaking. Though he knew the Greeks loved oratory—"excellency of speech"—he also knew such an influence would not strike deep enough to do the work he desired to accomplish. It was not admiration for himself that he was seeking but conversion to Christ and a change of character in his hearers. Eloquence itself was powerless to produce that. It might dazzle, excite, and give pleasure for a moment, but it would produce no lasting effect. Mere eloquence is like the light produced by a match applied to wood shavings. They burn with a sudden flash, blazing for an instant, and then go out without leaving either coals or heat behind.

Nor did he try the sophism prevalent at the time. Sophism is a degeneration of the philosophy and wisdom of the higher thinkers such as Socrates and Plato. The sophists had some disciples and exercised some influence, but they did not have the answer to the problem of sin. They could not save the souls of men (Beecher 1868, 1:13–16).

Having spoken about himself and how he felt when he came to Corinth, in 1 Corinthians 2:3, Paul proceeds in verse 4 to tell them and us how he preached. He was conscious of his own weakness, saying, "I was [or 'I became,' *egenomēn*] with you in weakness, and in fear, and in much trembling." But when it came to the message Paul preached, it was anything but weak. A man of God is most conscious of his own weakness in view of the responsibility of leading souls to Christ. The only thing that gives him courage to tackle the task is that he is giving forth God's own Word, at His command.

Dr. Westfield, Bishop of Bristol in the reign of Charles I, was so excellent a preacher that he was called "a born orator." Yet he was so conscious of his insufficiency that he never ascended the pulpit, even when he had been fifty years a preacher, without trembling. Preaching once before the King at Oxford, he fainted away, but His Majesty awaited his recovery, and then heard a sermon that powerfully moved him. The more conscious a preacher is of his weakness, the more powerful and effective may be the message he preaches.

Note how, in this entire passage of 1 Corinthians 2:1–5, Paul introduces each new thought with the connective conjunction *kai:*

Verse 1: "*And,* when I came unto you, brethren, I came not in the superiority of expression [*logou*] or wisdom"—that is, I came not trusting in oratory or human wisdom. This was his attitude of mind.

Verse 3: "*And* I became unto you in weakness, and in fear, and in much trembling." This was the consciousness Paul had of himself

Verse 4: "*And* my word or speech [*logos*] and my preaching was [this verb is not in the Greek text but is understood] not with enticing words of man's wisdom, but in demonstration of the Spirit and of power." This is the fervor and power of the heart in the Holy Spirit.

This conjunction (*kai,* "and") joins the three attitudes of Paul's mind, body, and heart or spirit. Here we have an example of how a preacher should tackle the task of proclaiming the gospel. He should not depend on his brilliant mind, though he may have one, but should recognize that in himself he is utterly weak and unable to effect the salvation of a single life. But he must also recognize the power of the Spirit of God working in and through his own spirit to effect a radical change in others. Mind, body, spirit—all three should be in the proper attitude as he executes his duty of proclaiming Christ and Him crucified.

As Paul entered Corinth, he might very well have raised his eyes to heaven and prayed as did George Whitefield,

> My life, my blood, I here present,
> If for Thy cause they may be spent.
> Fulfill Thy sovereign counsel, Lord,
> Thy will be done, Thy name adored.
> Give me Thy strength, O God of power;
> Then let winds blow, or thunders roar,
> Thy faithful witness will I be;
> 'Tis fixed: I can do all for Thee!

Use Plain Speech in Soulwinning

"And my speech and my preaching was not with enticing words of man's wisdom," declared the apostle Paul to the Corinthians. He brought forth the negative attitude of his spirit before he brought forth the positive. Before you can fill a vessel with something good, you must first empty it of anything that is evil. The verb "was not," used in the Authorized Version, does not occur in the Greek text, but is obviously understood.

The word translated "speech" is *logos,* the same word we find in 1 Corinthians 1:5 translated "utterance," in 1:17 translated "words" (plural), in 1:18 translated "preaching," and in 2:1 translated "speech." We must always keep in mind the basic meaning of the word *logos*. It comes from the verb *legō* (root, *leg*), meaning "to gather." When you speak, you use your mind, your intelligence (another meaning of the word *logos* from which we derive the word "logic"), to gather together words to express your thoughts. *Logos*, therefore, in its basic meaning, is the gathering together of words by using your mind to express a concept. Only logical beings *legōn*, "speak." It is the expression of thought through a collection of words.

Note that there are two other distinct Greek words that are translated as "speak, speech, word, etc.," but they have a different connotation. The first is the noun *rhēma*, along with its verb form *ereō* or *erō*, which means a specific word or saying, as in Luke 5:5. "At thy word," said Peter, "I will let down the net." That is, "on your specific instruction" I will do it.

The second word is the noun *lalia*, with its verb form *laleō*, which is speech that does not necessarily express one's thought processes. It is akin to the English word "lull," which derives one of its meanings from its resemblance to the bubbling sound made by small children, and thus by extension means "to prattle." When we want to refer to speech, we use the word *laleō* (see Kittel 1967).

Interestingly enough, this is the word that predominates in Paul's discussion of the Corinthian practice of speaking in an unknown tongue in 1 Corinthians 12 and 14 (see 12:3, 30; 13:1, 11; 14:2–6, 9). However, until now, whenever Paul referred to speaking or speech in connection with the gospel, he always used the words *legō* (1 Cor. 1:10, 12) and *logos* (1 Cor. 1:5, 17, 18; 2:1, 4). In 1 Corinthians 2:4, when Paul says, "And my preaching [*logos*] was not with enticing words of man's wisdom," he meant, "I did not use my mind to gather together words just to attract the attention and admiration of my hearers."

Words are tremendously important, and we must use our minds, of course, in their selection to convey a specific concept. But as we gather these words together in preparation for preaching the gospel, let us always keep our goal in mind. Why do we choose this word rather than another? Is it to show off our superior learning or to convey the meaning of the gospel with utmost clarity? Preacher, watch your choice of words.

Once that great Puritan preacher, Thomas Manton, had to speak before the Lord Mayor and Aldermen of London. He chose a subject in which he had an opportunity of displaying his learning and judgment. He was heard with admiration by the intelligent part of his audience, but as he was returning from dinner with the Lord Mayor, a poor man pulled him by the sleeve and asked if he was the gentleman that preached the sermon. He replied that he was. "Sir," said the man, "I came with the hopes of getting some good to my soul, but I was greatly disappointed, for I could not understand a great deal of what you said; you were quite above my comprehension." "Friend," said Dr. Manton, "if I have not given you a sermon, you have given me one. By the grace of God, I will not play the fool in such a manner again."

Preacher, if you have to choose between words that only some understand and admire you for, and words that all will understand with the distinct possibility of being led to the Savior, choose the latter. Sometimes the decision to write out your sermon and read it may have the subtle motivation of enabling you to choose more admirable words. When you speak extemporaneously you may use more common words. Though you may attract less admiration to yourself you may lead more souls to the Savior. Which is more important?

A man was asked what he thought of a sermon which he had just heard delivered and which had appeared to produce a great sensation among the congregation. His reply may suggest an important lesson to preachers. "Very fine, sir. It was very flowery, but a man cannot live upon flowers!"

In employing the word *logos* then, in 1 Corinthians 2:4, Paul meant, "My choice of words, the expression of my mind, was not with enticing words of man's wisdom." It was not to show off how much human wisdom he possessed. The *logos*, then, is the speech or the means of conveying the message. And that is why Paul adds, "and my preaching."

The word for "preaching" in Greek is *kērugma* (found in Matt. 12:41, Luke 11:32, Rom. 16:25, 1 Cor. 1:21; 2:4; 15:14, 2 Tim. 4:17, Titus 1:3). It may mean the act of proclaiming or the content of the proclamation. I believe that in 1 Corinthians 2:4 it refers both to the content of Paul's preaching and its delivery. "My delivery and my sermon were not with enticing words of man's wisdom." In fact, the word "sermon" in modern Greek can only be expressed by the word *kērugma*. Paul presented the message of the gospel in such a way, with such words, as not merely to obtain human assent or to gain an argument or win a point, but to win souls to Christ. Words can win a debate but will not necessarily change a human life.

John Wesley's preaching was marked by his constant use of the plainest, simplest words our language affords. Writing to one whose style was very high-sounding he said:

> When I had been a member of the University about ten years I wrote and talked much as you do now, but when I talked to plain people . . . I observed that they gaped and stared. This quickly obliged me to alter my style and adopt the language of those I spoke to; and yet there is a dignity in this simplicity which is not disagreeable to those of the highest rank." As another preacher said, "If you preach so that the simplest person in the audience can understand you, the most educated is also sure to get the message.

Preaching That Changes Lives

"Wouldn't it be wonderful," said a thoughtful woman of my acquaintance, "if everyone in the world were only interested in arriving at the truth, and not merely in winning an argument?" Wonderful, indeed—in private life, in politics, and in the pulpit.

The preacher in his choice of words and in the sermon itself should never have as his purpose what human wisdom seeks to do—merely to persuade people to agree with him or to please him. That is as far as human wisdom can go—to persuade others of the correctness of a certain point. But that is not what a sermon should seek to do. Its goal should not be to win agreement but to win souls to Christ.

"And my speech and my preaching [or sermon] was not with enticing words of man's wisdom," declared the apostle Paul. The preposition "with" in Greek is *en,* the basic meaning of which is "in." "My mind and my sermon were not presented in persuasive words of wisdom" would be a better translation of the Greek text of 1 Corinthians 2:4. In more recent critical Greek texts the adjective "human," *anthrōpinēs,* found in the *Textus Receptus* from which the King James Version was translated, is missing. The word *sophias,* "of wisdom," refers to human wisdom anyway. The word translated "enticing" in the KJV is *peithoi(s)* in Greek, in the plural to make it agree with *logois.* The adjective *peithos* is found only here in 1 Corinthians 2:4, but the verb *peithō* occurs more than fifty times in the New Testament. The verb means "to persuade, to convince." If we take the reading as *en peithois sophias logois,* the word *peithois* is an adjective and the translation is "in persuasive words of wisdom." If we take the reading as *en peithoi sophias,* then *peithoi* is a noun and the translation is "with the persuasive art of wisdom." As far as the interpretation of the sentence is concerned, it makes no difference which reading we accept. In either case Paul is stating that his preaching does not derive its power to convince from the rhetorical art of human wisdom.

In fact, Paul is in another realm entirely. There is a contrast, an antithesis, between the purpose of human wisdom and mere persuasive words and the preaching of the gospel. "But [I came to you] in the demonstration of the Spirit and of power." Persuasion is achieved through the careful selection of words. But conversion is accomplished through the Spirit, which is the power of God unto salvation.

The word translated "demonstration" is *apodeixei* in Greek. This is the only place in the New Testament where this word occurs as a noun. As a verb (*apodeiknumi*) it is found in Acts 2:22, translated "approved"—better "proven"; 25:7, 1 Corinthians 4:9 translated "set forth"; and 2 Thessalonians 2:4 translated "shewing himself"; or better, "proving himself," that He is God. *Apodeixis* means "proof." In modern Greek the word is used very commonly with this meaning. The paper someone gives you as a receipt for anything is *apodeixis*.

The evidence that Paul's message was not made up of nice words to tantalize the hearers was the changed lives in Corinth. They were changed by the Spirit and power. The proof of the effectiveness of any sermon is not the heads that nod assent or the tongues that utter flattery but the hearts that are repentant and changed by the power of the gospel. A young preacher in his first pastorate was standing at the door greeting his people when one woman said, "That was a fine sermon, Pastor. I enjoyed it very much." "That is not what I want to hear," remarked the pastor with more honesty than tact. "I want to hear that people change their lives as a result."

Whenever a soul is saved in a meeting where I have preached, I need not go back to the words that I uttered to find the cause, but instead I praise God who worked salvation in the human heart through His Spirit. Because of its contextual usage, I believe that the genitive *pneumatos*, "of spirit," though not preceded by the definite article, refers not to the spirit of man but to the Holy Spirit. And where the Holy Spirit is at work, power is released. Whenever or wherever we see souls saved, it is the proof of the presence of the Holy Spirit and of the power of the gospel.

The word translated "of power" is *dunameōs*, the same word we find in Romans 1:16, "For I am not ashamed of the gospel of Christ: for it is the power of God unto salvation to everyone that believeth; to the Jew first, and also to the Greek." Never be tempted to give the credit for the conversion of souls to your beautifully worded and constructed sermons or to your persuasive oratory. You and I cannot possibly lead a soul to Christ apart from the Holy Spirit, for it is His power that does it all. Give Him the glory. If you try to persuade people in your own power, by your own words, they may respond, but unless it is a product of the Spirit's action, their response is a mere profession devoid of any real change in the life of the individual.

George Whitefield had just finished one of his sermons when a man came reeling up to him and said, "How do you do, Mr. Whitefield?" Whitefield replied, "I do not know you, sir." "Don't know me! Why you converted me so many years ago in such a place." "I should not wonder," replied Mr. Whitefield. "You look like one of my converts, for if the Lord had converted you, you would have been a sober man."

In the business of fishing for men, it is not your skill or fine equipment that produces results; it is the power of the Holy Spirit. A fisherman who had all the equipment that the best sporting goods store could sell him was having no success. Seeing a country lad with a stick and a bent pin for a hook, he smiled condescendingly, then did a double take. On the bank beside the boy lay a fine string of trout.

"How is it that I cannot catch any?" the man inquired. "Because you do not keep yourself out of sight," the boy replied.

That is the secret of fishing for men as well as trout. Preach Christ and Him crucified, and send the people away talking about Him instead of praising you.

LESSONS:

1. Having said in 1 Corinthians 2:3 how he felt weak in coming to Corinth, Paul proceeds to tell in verse 4 how he preached an anything but weak message. For, the thing which gives a man courage to tackle the task of leading souls to Christ is that he is giving forth God's own Word, at His command.

2. The Greek word *kai,* translated "and," joins the three attitudes of Paul's mind, body, heart, and spirit by beginning verses 1, 3, and 4. All three should be in the proper attitude as one executes his duty of proclaiming Christ and Him crucified.

3. Preachers should watch their choice of words so that they may convey the meaning of the gospel with utmost clarity, and not seek to show off superior learning.

4. Paul presented the gospel with such words, as not merely to obtain human assent, or to gain an argument, or to win a point, but to win souls to Christ.

5. Persuasion is achieved through the careful selection of words, but conversion is accomplished through the Holy Spirit, which is the power of God unto salvation.

6. The proof of the effectiveness of any sermon is not the heads that nod assent or the tongues that utter flattery but the hearts that are repentant and changed by the power of the gospel.

1 Cor. 2:5

How Faith Goes Farther Than Reason

That your faith should not stand in the wisdom of men, but in the power of God.

What Is True Faith?

We hear a good deal of talk about faith nowadays. Your doctor, lawyer, teacher, parent, or child may ask you to "have faith" in him. Leaders of various religious persuasions ask you to "have faith" in their teachings. People in all walks of life, Christian or not, will assure you that they "have faith."

Faith may be mental or it may be spiritual. When you say you believe the Christian faith, what do you really mean? Is it that you merely give assent to the correctness of what God has done in sending His Son to die for sinful man? In order to bring you to that position, a preacher must use every argumentative power he possesses. But that does not mean that your life has been permeated by God, that your soul has been redeemed, that you have become a child of God. That involves not mere consent of the mind but transformation of the heart, the new birth.

Human wisdom, logic, may cause you to believe intellectually in God. But the same reason and human wisdom may destroy that kind of mental faith. What turns you to it can turn you away from it. But if your faith comes to you through Christ and

Him crucified, applied by the power of the Holy Spirit, then you have a living faith that no human wisdom or reasoning can destroy. The faith that people are said to lose is mere mental assent.

Living, true faith in Christ, on the other hand, stands on the basis of divine power, a supernatural revelation of God to both understanding and heart, powerful enough to take possession of both, and not liable to be shaken by any other force.

Paul wanted the Corinthians to understand why, in his preaching to them, he did not employ human wisdom but was wholly dependent upon the Spirit of God. "Human wisdom could never have made you what you have now become, new creatures in Christ," he told them in effect. "I preached to you the way I did, not with persuasive words of human wisdom, so 'that your faith should not stand in the wisdom of men, but in the power of God'" (1 Cor. 2:5).

If Paul had wanted to make people agree with him, he would have propounded a philosophy, and he could have made adherents of his school of philosophy, as many philosophers have done before and after Paul. But that was not his purpose. "So that" (*hina*) expresses the purpose of his preaching and the explanation of the manner and content of his preaching. "So that your faith may not be in the wisdom of men." In Greek it is the same preposition *en* here in verse 5 as in verse 4. "And my speech and my preaching was not 'in' [*en*] persuasive words of human wisdom, but 'in' [*en*] demonstration [proof of the Spirit and of power, so that your faith may not be 'in' [*en*] the wisdom of men but 'in' [*en*] the power of God." Clearly Paul indicated that there could be faith in the area of human wisdom, as well as the faith that the Corinthians possessed, which was the result of the transforming power of the Spirit of God.

People are ever confounding the two. Faith, they think, is simply intellectual belief produced by pure reasoning, leading men to act accordingly. They think that religious faith is wrought exactly as a proof in mathematics, or logic, or in a court of law. It rests upon the evidence of facts, and reasonings about them, inferences drawn from them, and certain conclusions reached. It is simply the intellect in its ordinary processes dealing with religious things. The man who rejects Christianity does it on this ground. "I cannot," he says, "find historical evidence sufficient to convince me. I cannot reason out a demonstrative proof of Christianity; therefore I refuse to believe it true." Because faith cannot stand in the wisdom of men, it cannot, he thinks, stand at all.

Now clearly, according to the apostle's thought, this is not the true ground of Christian faith; it stands in something he calls "the power of God." What is it? What is the difference? What is the domain of faith as distinguished from the domain of reason? What is the proof of faith as distinguished from the proof which mere reasoning establishes? The distinction is vital. Whether we are justified in believing in Christ or whether we can be Christians depends on it.

Proof of course is mighty important. "Prove it and I shall believe it," people say. We know things by different kinds of proof. If I put my finger into the fire, it proves that fire burns. If I am hungry, I crave food. If I have a fever, I feel discomfort and pain. If I hear music, it delights me. If I smell perfume or taste sweets, I am gratified. This is what is called the proof of the senses. It is the proof that my physical body furnishes concerning things that appeal to it. I do not reason about them. No moral or spiritual sympathies are called into existence. I prove them by purely physical sensations, exactly as an animal does which has no ability to reason. So much for proof of the senses.

But there is also the evidence or the proof of reason. If a man tells me that the earth moves around the sun, that two and two make four, that a whole is greater than any of its parts, that two sides of a right angled triangle are greater than its third side, that a process of logic is conclusive, that certain methods are wiser and better than others, I believe on the evidence of my reason. My senses have nothing to do with the proof, nor do my religious feelings. It is a process of pure reason. An irrational animal could not prove anything in this way. A rational man must believe on such evidence—that is his nature. This is a second method of proof, then, the proof of one's reason.

However, there is a third method of proof that we shall consider in our next study—the proof that appeals to the heart, to our moral nature, to our God-consciousness. I believe it is no less valid than the proof of the senses or the proof of reason.

Does Faith Contradict Reason?

How do you size up your fellowmen? You probably follow much the same procedure that I do. When I see moral qualities in a man, when he speaks to me, lets me see his feelings, I instinctively receive impressions concerning him. I may say he is a kind man, a true man, a reverential man. I do not know enough about him to reason out these conclusions, but there is something in me that recognizes these qualities in him. If he is a hypocrite and pretends to have qualities that he actually has not, he may deceive me, but that does not affect the validity of this method of proof. Why, life would be impossible if we could not trust men until we had collected all the evidence about them. We are always trusting men whom we know little about because of the moral judgment we form of them.

Again, a man makes a statement to me; or twelve men sit on a jury to listen to statements—to witnesses flatly contradicting each other, perhaps. They are trusted and required to form a judgment; and mainly by exercising their moral instincts. This is moral proof, the proof of probability. The thing does not appeal to the senses. I have no facts upon which I can reason out a conclusion. I judge by the instincts and sympathies of my moral nature. It is my moral nature simply seeing with its own proper organ of vision; for if there is an eye of the physical body capable of discerning sensible things, if there is an eye of the reason capable of discerning intellectual truth, I believe there is also an eye of the soul capable of discerning spiritual truth and holiness. The vision of sense, the vision of the understanding, do not aid it; it is pure, direct, spiritual perception, as direct and certain as light to the eye, or truth to the understanding.

Now, this distinction of different kinds of proof will carry us a long way in understanding the domain of faith as distinguished from that of intellectual wisdom. When God speaks spiritual truth to me, He does not appeal to my physical senses— to my sight, or touch, or hearing. He does not appeal to my intellectual reason, as the multiplication table does, or a proof in logic does. He appeals directly to my spiritual sensitivities. Is not this spiritually true? Is it not spiritually pure? Is it not spiritually suitable? And my spiritual sense responds to light, as the eye of the understanding responds to intellectual truth, as the heart responds to love. Men who are "of the truth," who are susceptible to the truth, who are truth-loving, respond to spiritual and moral truth when they see it.

However, a great deal of confusion is caused by the effort of men to interchange these different methods of proof. "I can believe nothing I cannot prove," says the materialistic man of science. Quite true. No one should. But what kind of proof does he mean? "I mean proof that comes by the processes of reason." But not all things are proved in that way. Material things do not require proofs of reason. Suppose an animal were capable of speech and that it declared, "I will believe nothing I cannot prove by my senses, nothing I cannot taste, touch, see, hear, or smell." That is fine. But then it turns and says to you, "I will not believe in your mathematical astronomy, your historic geology, your subtle chemistry." Is it not as much justified in denying your rational proof as you are in denying my spiritual proof? Your rational proof belongs to a higher nature than the animal's, whereas my spiritual proof belongs to a higher nature than mere reason.

What can reason do with spiritual, moral qualities? You cannot reason out right and wrong; you cannot by reason prove love or purity or goodness; you can only feel them intuitively. Your reason can do very little in accounting for the universe. When it has dealt with physical nature, and with all that pertains to the purely intellectual domain, there remains a whole world of moral things that it cannot account for or even touch. They are there, whether it will deal with them or not. The scientific materialist tells us that he has explored the domain of nature but cannot find God. As well may the surgeon conducting a postmortem tell us that he cannot find the pure patriot, the loving father in the body he is examining. How can anyone detect spiritual, moral qualities by physical tests?

We are always trying to get above the domain of mere matter into that of reason, from the lower to the higher. The painter and the poet idealize nature, changing actual color and form into glorious ideals. The philosopher uses them for the creation of a science. The economist uses them for an economy of social life. Even so we are always trying to get above the domain of reason into the domain of faith. It is our instinct, the necessity of our nature, to think about right and wrong, good and evil, to form moral judgments about things, to attribute spiritual values. We cannot regard them as mere matter, as mechanical laws. All the reasoning in the world cannot induce us to ignore conscience, to deny providence, to disallow religion, to exclude God. We are so made that we must seek God. We are always trying to translate the material into the spiritual. There is, of course, another tendency that is always dragging the spiritual down to the sensual, but all men agree to call this wrong moral feeling; Christianity calls it sin.

What, then, is faith in the power of God as Paul speaks of it? It is that quality of our spiritual nature that, when it hears God's truth, sees God's purity, feels God's love, simply and implicitly believes it, trusts it, confides in it. It does not wait for reason to prove it, anymore than the eye waits for reason to prove light, or the heart for processes of reason to prove love. Faith by its very nature takes knowledge of spiritual things. It alone has an ear to listen to them; it alone has a heart to feel them.

"But," someone may say, "does not this make faith irrational? Is not faith without reason fanaticism? Can faith contradict reason?" Certainly not. There must be reason, intelligent understanding, in the whole process of faith. Faith does not contradict reason; it simply goes farther than reason can go, sees things that reason cannot see, feels things that reason cannot feel.

When the truth of God is spoken to me, first my senses are exercised; if audibly spoken, my hearing; if written, my seeing. Next my reason is exercised; it judges the meaning of the words, of the thought, then delivers the sentiment to my spiritual faculty. I then perceive it as spiritually true, spiritually pure, suitable, and precious. Simple reason could not pronounce upon this, but my religious heart does, my conscience, my sensibilities.

Why You Cannot Discover God by Reason

Reason and faith are not opposed to each other, as some people seem to think. Rather they are different faculties for seeing, different methods of proving. When reason proves a thing, it acts upon phenomena as truths, and deduces from them its conclusions. When faith proves a thing, it judges its spiritual qualities, its spiritual truth, purity, and goodness. Faith judges things that reason has no faculty for judging; it judges the spiritual things of the soul, things that are unseen, that senses cannot recognize at all, that the reason cannot demonstrate. Faith does not contradict reason, anymore than reason contradicts sense. It simply goes beyond it, testifying where reason has no faculty.

If I tell you of the existence of God, your senses cannot recognize Him, your reason cannot demonstrate Him, but your soul, your spiritual nature, can confess His existence just as your heart confesses love. All that reason can prove confirms such faith, but your faith itself is an instinct of your spiritual nature.

If I tell you of the incarnation of Christ, neither sense nor reason can prove it, but your spiritual consciousness can testify that it is precisely what your condition needed. It is so congruous, so wonderful, so glorious that it must be true. It is a moral necessity. And everything that reason can determine simply confirms such instinctive belief in this great revelation.

If I tell you of the atonement, the death of the incarnate Son for human guilt, reason cannot prove it. It can be known only by divine revelation, but it is so wonderfully suited for human sin, it so perfectly and marvelously solves the problem of guilt, it so satisfies righteousness and love, justice and mercy, it so wonderfully maintains the righteousness of the divine Law, and provides for the holy forgiveness of transgressors, that it is like a light shining into a terrible darkness. Your whole soul leaps forward to it. You need not wait for proofs of it; light proves itself, and all after-reasonings simply illustrate and confirm the instinctive conclusions of your soul.

It is the same with the regeneration of the Holy Spirit, with the resurrection of Christ and the immortal life that He gives. Reason cannot demonstrate them. Jesus Christ simply declares them, speaks them as great truths of God; the souls of men hear Him and believe Him. They are truths that solve all problems, meet all necessities. They are revelations of light; they are words of life. That is why the declaration of these truths is called *kērugma* in Greek, "sermon, telling forth, heralding." We do not argue about the gospel; we declare it. Reason could not have discovered anything like it. Reason could not construct any argument that could prove it. But when God has revealed it to the eye of the soul, your reason confirms it; every test that it can apply establishes it. Reason alone could not discover the truth, but it can assure itself that it is true.

This is what Paul means by saying, "Faith does not stand in the wisdom of men, but in the power of God." The things of faith cannot be proved by human reasoning: faith stands in the revelation of God, who reveals the things of faith to your soul, makes it see them and experience them with a divine power of conviction. In this way, the apostle tells us we realize Christ crucified. We see the divine fact of Jesus Christ's incarnation and death.

Paul did not come to Corinth to argue about the gospel; he came to declare it. It was in that sense a simple though stupendous fact that he had to proclaim. He had to tell the Corinthians that God had sent Jesus Christ into the world to die for the sin of man. Men knew all about sin; Paul did not need to prove they were sinful. Men earnestly craved forgiveness, to know what they must do to be saved. He did not need to reason about that. Paul took for granted men's sin and their need for salvation, and he simply declared the great, unique fact that God's Son was crucified for sin, that "Christ Jesus came into the world to save sinners." That was all he said, but that was enough. Men at once understood it; they knew what the great sacrifice meant. Paul simply made it clear that the great sacrifice had been offered.

He felt himself inadequate to this great testimony; he was timid, full of fear. He knew most men would scorn and reject it, but he was bent only upon making it clear. His "speech and preaching was not with persuasive words of wisdom," like the teachings of the philosophers. It was simply a testimony to a most colossal fact, and a demonstration of its spiritual wisdom and power. He had to show the great fact of eternal significance, that God had accomplished man's redemption through Christ crucified, and that in this great transaction the very thought and heart, the very spirit and power of God were expressed. It was full of spiritual power to subdue and save men. Thus, receiving his testimony to the divine fact, the faith of those men "stood not in the wisdom of men, but in the power of God" (Allon 1888, 33:136–37).

Several learned men once tried to persuade a great scholar to believe in Christianity, but all their labor was in vain. A plain honest person referred not so much to logical reasoning as to the work of the Holy Spirit; and the scholar exclaimed, "When I heard no more than human reason, I opposed it with human reason, but when I heard the Spirit, I was obliged to surrender." Thus it is that, trusting to their own wisdom, the wisest are lost; while those who are taught of the Spirit know the way of God in truth.

Omar Khayyam, the Persian poet, once wrote:

> Myself when young did eagerly frequent
> Doctor and Saint, and heard great argument
> About it and about: but evermore
> Came out by the same door where in I went.

That is what happens when men depend on argument to convince the unbeliever of the truth of the gospel. But when the Holy Spirit speaks to a man's heart, He brings conviction of the truth and a change of heart and life.

LESSONS:

1. The faith that people are said to lose is mere mental assent. Living, true faith in Christ, on the other hand, stands on the basis of divine power, a supernatural revelation of God to both understanding and heart, powerful enough to take possession of both, and not liable to be shaken by any other force.

2. Three methods of proof include: proof of the senses; proof of one's reason; and the proof that appeals to the heart, to our moral nature, and to our God-consiousness.

3. While rational proof belongs to a higher nature than the animal's, spiritual proof belongs to a higher nature than mere reason.

4. All the reasoning in the world cannot induce us to ignore conscience, to deny providence, to disallow religion, or to exclude God. We are so made that we must seek God.

5. Faith does not contradict reason, but simply goes farther than reason can go.

6. Paul did not come to Corinth to argue about the gospel. He came to declare it.

1 Cor. 2:6 | *Why So Many Mysteries in the Christian Faith?*

Howbeit we speak wisdom among them that are perfect: yet not the wisdom of this world, nor of the princes of this world, that come to nought.

How to Acquire True Wisdom

Two men returning from India got into a conversation. One was a sportsman and the other a missionary. "I have been in India for twenty-five years, and I never saw one of the natives converted as you Christians claim," said the sportsman. "That is strange," said the missionary. "Did you ever see a tiger?" "Hundreds of them," was the reply, "and I have shot dozens of them." "Well, I have been in India for many years," said the missionary. "but I have never seen a tiger. But under the power of the gospel of Christ I have seen hundreds of the natives of India turn to the Savior." You see, one was looking for tigers, the other was looking for souls.

A philosopher in Corinth might have confronted the apostle Paul with the same kind of objection. "I have not seen any of these people you call saved." Well, he did not take the trouble to look for them. Paul could have pointed to many of them. Anyone who doubts that the lives of men can be transformed by the power of God should go looking for them in the right places; he will be amazed.

The first impression of the skeptic as he looks at a believer in Christ is that he is deficient in wisdom. But that is a very superficial judgment. A little investigation will show that a great many wise and well-educated persons are believers, as well as those of humbler attainments. In fact, Paul declares, believers are the wisest people possible, but their wisdom is different from the wisdom that characterizes this age. "Howbeit we speak wisdom among them that are perfect: yet not the wisdom of this world, nor of the princes of this world, that come to nought" (1 Cor. 2:6). In verses 1–5 Paul told the Corinthian Christians that he came to them in fear and trembling preaching salvation through the crucified Christ. He did not want their faith to be mere mental assent but a change of heart and life. Such changed lives can always be found by those who seek them.

Furthermore, Paul wanted the Corinthian Christians to realize that though their faith was not the product of human wisdom and reasoning, it did not lack real wisdom. The Greek word translated "howbeit" at the beginning of verse 6 is the particle *de* which might better be translated as the contrasting conjunction "but." "But we speak wisdom among them." In the Greek text the verse actually begins with the word "wisdom." Literally it reads, "Wisdom we speak among them that are perfect, but wisdom not of this world." Paul contrasts the wisdom of the world with the wisdom of God, as he did so masterfully in the first chapter. The wisdom of men is that which originates in the minds of men, while the wisdom of God is that which originates with God and is received by men through faith. Actually, this wisdom that man receives by faith is not an idea but a person, the Lord Jesus Christ.

When the Lord Jesus entered His hometown of Nazareth one Sabbath, He began to teach in the synagogue. "Many hearing him were astonished, saying, From whence hath this man these things? and what wisdom is this which is given unto him, that even such mighty works are wrought by his hands?" (Mark 6:2). The wisdom of God was most manifestly operative in what Christ did and was. The partial personification of wisdom in Proverbs 8:22–31 made it easier to conceive of wisdom as incarnate in Christ. The basic thesis of Paul in this Corinthian epistle is that, when man receives Christ, the power of God makes the natural fool who mistakenly thinks himself wise into a really wise person. If you possess Christ, God's incarnate wisdom, you are automatically wise. In all that really matters, a born-again believer is far wiser than the most brilliant unconverted person in the world.

What is the first and basic truth that a believer accepts? That God is the Creator of the universe. That is wisdom. Allow me to illustrate. Here is NASA. It places in orbit a weather satellite called Nimbus, which contains 57,359 parts and 2,000 units having to do with experiments. The largest U.S. orbiting satellite [in 1974], the Orbiting Astronomical Observatory (OAO), weighing more than two tons, contains 238,000 parts, not including those prepared for scientific experiments. Someone asked NASA how many of those parts would be needed if the goal was only to achieve and maintain its exact orbit. The reply was, "All 238,000."

You may have seen the mighty Saturn V, a stupendously powerful machine, as big as a 36-story skyscraper, yet unthinkably delicate, ready for launching. Created out of metals and plastic, it is built with the precision of a fine watch. Sections of its fuel-tank walls have been machined down to 80/1000ths of an inch. It took five years to build. To assemble this incredible construction required the knowhow of thousands of firms and the energies of thousands of thinking people. How would you react to the public press if they reported that the Saturn V had really assembled itself out in space, completely by chance, from the jettisoned hardware of some unknown civilization of a past age? Do you not think NASA's feelings might be a little hurt—after all that work? And would not you conclude that you would have been reading a pretty tall tale? Yet that is exactly what some supposedly wise men of the world constantly teach in our schools, that the world put itself together by sheer chance. How foolish can human wisdom get?

If you want to become wise, believe in God. Receive His wisdom by appropriating the work of Christ into your heart and life. That is Paul's thesis as he writes to the Corinthians. He has already stated it in 1 Corinthians 1:23, 24: "But we preach Christ crucified, unto the Jews a stumbling block, and unto the Greeks foolishness, but unto them which are called [*klētois*, meaning those effectively called, who have received Christ the crucified], both Jews and Greeks. Christ the power of God, and the wisdom of God."

The verb Paul uses in 1 Corinthians 2:6, translated "speak" in the phrase, "Howbeit we speak wisdom among them that are perfect," is *laloumen* in Greek. He uses it three times in this passage, here, and in verses 7 and 13: "But we speak the wisdom of God in a mystery. . . . Which things also we speak, not in the words which man's wisdom teacheth." In all three instances he also uses the plural pronoun "we," by which he means himself and any other preacher of the Word. Primarily, however, he means himself, as we can readily see from 1 Corinthians 3:1. where he reverts to the first person singular: "And I, brethren, could not speak [*lalēsai*, the same Greek word] unto you as unto spiritual."

The word *laleō* (I speak) stands in contrast to the verb *legō*. It is used in contrast to silence. It also means merely to make sounds without their necessarily expressing thought. (This is the meaning of the word constantly used by Paul in chapter 14 in regard to speaking with tongues, making sounds without necessarily expressing thought.) In this instance and context, what Paul means by the use of this verb is that we communicate God's wisdom without necessarily having to understand or explain it. We simply declare it as wisdom incapable of any human explanation. This fits in beautifully with another word in this passage, "mystery," a fact that defies explanation. That is what the wisdom of God is, and we must recognize it as such. Then we shall declare it in spite of the fact that we do not fully understand it. But declare it we must, and so we shall when we receive Jesus Christ, who is the wisdom of God unto us.

Why does Paul proclaim God's wisdom, embodied in the person of Christ, as light that is treasured in the sun? Chapter 19 of William Arnot's *Laws from Heaven for Life on Earth* includes discussion on Proverbs 3:13 which states, "Happy is the man that findeth wisdom, and the man that getteth understanding." Arnot writes:

> Saving wisdom is a thing to be "found" and "gotten:" it is not required of us that we create it. We could not plan, we could not execute a way of righteous redemption for sinners. . . . This is all his own doing; and it is all done. . . . When we are saved, it is by "finding" a salvation already complete, and being ourselves "complete in him."
>
> . . . It comes not in sparks from our own intellect in collision with other human minds. It is a light from heaven, above the brightness of this world's sun [99, 100].

Why Some Cannot Understand God's Dealings with Them

Have you ever doubted the wisdom of God? Have you ever thought that if you were He, you would have done things differently? Perhaps you are somewhat like that man who rested under an oak tree and wondered, "Why should such a large tree produce such a small fruit as the acorn?" Then looking at a nearby gourd-vine with a fruit weighing many pounds he continued,

"How singular that so small a plant should grow such large fruit! If I had been God I would have put the small fruit on the small plant, and the large gourd on this great oak." Just then an acorn fell on his head, and the thought flashed through his mind, "If that had been the gourd, I would probably by this time have been a corpse." He immediately fell to his knees to ask forgiveness of his Creator. He realized that God knew what He was doing.

In 1 Corinthians 1 and 2 the apostle Paul makes the point that an unbeliever looks at the wisdom of God as foolishness, both in creation and redemption. But a perfect man, that is, a mature believer, accepts whatever God has done as not capable of being improved upon. Such understanding is wisdom from God. But this understanding comes to the believer gradually. A spiritually mature person accepts God as the all-wise Creator and Redeemer. The babe in Christ may have doubts about His wisdom. In 1 Corinthians 2:6 Paul says in effect, "We declare God's wisdom without questioning or trying to explain it." And to whom or among whom does he declare it? "Them that are perfect." What does he mean by that expression?

The Greek word for the "perfect ones" mentioned here is *teleiois,* an adjectival noun derived from the substantive *telos,* which means "end, goal." *Teleios* is the one who reaches the goal that he or someone else sets for him. Thus, if you want to be perfect before God, you must reach the goal He sets for you. If you want to be perfect in your own eyes you must reach the goal you set for yourself.

Teleois should not be taken to mean faultless or sinless when applied to man. In relation to man the word "perfect" is relative, whereas in relation to God it is absolute. A good illustration of that is Matthew 5:48. "Be ye therefore perfect [*teleioi*], even as your Father which is in heaven is perfect [*teleios*]." It would be blasphemy to conclude that what our Lord meant here is that in this life a man can become all that God is, can achieve His holiness, His omnipotence, His omniscience. We do not become little gods walking around on earth. What the Lord meant is that a child of God should aim to be faithful in reaching the goal set by God, producing the fruits that He meant us to produce. A perfect child of God is a mature child of God in contrast to a babe in Christ.

When we are born into the physical world, we are, in one sense, perfect. All our organs are formed, and we are potentially all that our Creator meant us to be. But in order to realize our full adult potential we must fulfill all the conditions for growth: eating, exercising, working, resting. A baby cannot possibly understand the wisdom of his parents in making him fulfill these conditions for growth. Only as he grows and matures does he come to understand them better.

Exactly the same thing happens in our spiritual relationship with God. If we remain babes in Christ, we cannot possibly understand and accept God's wisdom with the same capacity that a mature Christian can. Would you try to explain to a baby the mystery of his metabolism? He lacks the capacity to understand it. Even so, if you remain a babe in Christ, God must withhold from you a fuller revelation of His wisdom in creation, redemption, providence, and all His other activities.

The "perfect ones" of 1 Corinthians 2:6 stand in contrast to the "babes" of chapter 3, verse 1. Look at 1 Corinthians 14:20, where the contrast is most apparent. "Brethren, be not children in understanding: howbeit in malice be ye children, but in understanding be men." The Greek word translated "men" here is *teleioi*, "perfect, mature, grown-up." The *teleioi*, grown-up adults, are contrasted with the children or babes. *Teleioi*, "perfect," in 1 Corinthians 2:6 is synonymous with *pneumatikois*, "spiritual ones," in 1 Corinthians 3:1. The more spiritual you are, the more mature and spiritually grown-up, the more of the wisdom of God can be proclaimed to you. Not all Christians have the capacity to understand God equally. Their understanding of Him is proportionate to their spiritual growth. If you feel that God has withheld His deep wisdom from you, it could be because you have withheld from Him your obedience and implicit faith.

Just go back to the illustration of the child. His parents subject him to certain ways of life. He may have to obey, but the family relationship is so much better when he is able to understand why his parents want him to act in certain ways. In the same manner, you and I have to submit to God's wise interventions in our lives. But our relationship with Him becomes much more precious and satisfying when we are able to understand to a greater degree the reasons behind His dealings with us. The closer we are to the heart of God the clearer we hear His voice of wisdom.

Take the case of Bill. He comes to the alley where for years he has parked his car, only to find a ticket on it. He fumes and fusses because there was no sign prohibiting parking in that area. Nevertheless, he pays his fine and resolves never to park his car there again. Still, he cannot understand the reason for it. Some days later, however, he has his answer. During a windstorm, a mammoth oak has fallen right across the place where he had been parking his car. Had it been in its accustomed place, it would have been smashed. Thanks to the ticket that cost him three dollars it was not there.

Of course, it pleases God sometimes never to explain to us the reasons for many of His actions in our lives. But Paul maintains that the more mature we become as Christians the more God will reveal to us.

How Much Power Do the Rulers of This World Exercise Over Christians?

That forthright English clergyman, Dr. R. W. Dale, made this response to a young preacher who insisted that ministers must preach relevantly, to the times. "Young man, do not preach to the times. Go and preach to broken hearts, and you will preach relevantly and to the eternities."

We preachers are so apt to be taken up by what pertains to time instead of that which is eternal. We like to sound wise to our listeners. We tend to become brainwashed by the wisdom of our times. Paul may have faced such dangers when he encountered the philosophizing Greeks in Corinth. That is why he wants to make clear what kind of wisdom he is declaring, the "wisdom which is not of this world, nor of the rulers of this world, that come to nought" (1 Cor. 2:6).

The word translated "world" in verses 6 to 8 is *aiōn* in Greek, which means "age," and refers to time rather than space or matter. In an ethical sense it refers to the course and current of this world's affairs. *Aiōn* is a time period, short or long. Paul wanted to call attention to the fact that the wisdom of men had nothing of eternity in it. It belonged to the times but might not survive them. Human wisdom is changeable while divine wisdom is eternal. Like God, it does not change with the times. God's truth remains forever; that, therefore, is what we should preach.

A critic told a renowned evangelist, "Your preaching has put Christianity back one hundred years." The evangelist replied, "That is not back far enough. We must go back to the cross of Christ and to the 'faith which was once delivered to the saints.'"

Times change; God and His wisdom are eternal. It is said that it took 5,000 years for man's knowledge to double the first time. The last time it took only 15 years. It is inconceivable that doctors and scientists today would use the same textbooks their fathers used. Our new discoveries have rendered many of the old ones obsolete. However, there is an eternity about God's creation, redemption, and wisdom. Adam breathed oxygen and so do we. The course of our earth remains the same. Do you realize that in its huge elliptical orbit around the sun, it travels about

588,000,000 miles, at 67,000 miles an hour? It is staggering to realize that this planet closes its yearly voyage without the loss of a thousandth of a second in thousands of years! How can our wisdom compare with the eternal wisdom of God!

Paul's contention was that the wisdom of this age is sinful because it leaves God out. Therefore it cannot point the way to man's salvation. Since salvation is an eternal matter, it cannot be accomplished by temporal means. The transforming power of the gospel has changed people of all ages at all times. There is absolutely no need to change the formula. Man may have made outward advances, but inwardly he is the same sinful creature he has always been since the day he chose to sin and be separated from God.

A little boy asked, "Why is it that when I open a marigold it dies, but if God does it, it is so beautiful?" Before anyone could answer him, he said, "I know! It is because God always works from the inside." That is God's wise way of working with men—from the inside. Men with "deceitful and desperately wicked" hearts cannot be changed by outward reformation, by any philosophy of man, by any system of our times. Their basic need is for inward cleansing.

God's wisdom stands above man's because it is eternal. But Paul goes on to say that the wisdom of God that he proclaimed was not that of the rulers of this age either—those who were becoming inactive or about to perish. Let us carefully consider the meaning of this last phrase. Paul says first of all that those who rule this age are ruling temporarily. God allows them to rule, but not forever. The Authorized Version translates the word *archontōn* as "princes." But a prince is not always a ruler; he inherits power, but may not actually be given the opportunity to exercise it. *Archō*, in Greek, means "to rule, to exercise authority over others." In other words, Paul asserts that those who rule our age, the age of sin and grace, do not possess the same wisdom—call it philosophy of life if you like as the children of God. We as Christians are temporarily subject to their rule; nevertheless we are not their slaves. They may rule over and even persecute us, but it is Christ who indwells us and is the Supreme Ruler of our lives. It was that mystic saint of God, Madame Guyon, who in prison wrote these words:

> Strong are the walls around me
>   That hold me all the day,
> But they who thus have bound me
>   Cannot keep God away:
> My very dungeon walls are dear,
>   Because the God I love is here.

The next word we should note is *katargoumenōn*, "them [the rulers] that come to nought." This is the genitive plural participle, present passive, of the verb *katargeō;* which means "to render inactive, to condemn to inactivity," hence to destroy as far as their role of rulership is concerned. It is interesting that Paul uses the present participle, "them that are being rendered inactive now and will continue to be rendered inactive." Paul was not merely looking forward to the day when as a result of the direct intervention of God at Christ's Second Coming "he shall have put down [*katargēsē*, the same verb in the aorist active subjunctive, indicating in this context an action once for all in the future] all rule [*archēn*, basically the same word as *archontas*, 'rulers,'] and all authority and power" (1 Cor. 15:24; Zodhiates *Conquering* 1970, 354, 355, 412, 764). He wanted these Corinthian Christians, many of whom must have been suffering at the hands of these worldly rulers, not only to look forward to their future redemption from them as a result of Christ's intervention at His Second Coming, but also to be comforted by the fact that this was in process already. "They are being canceled out now." The rulers of this age are robbed of their power over the Christian.

This same verb is also used in regard to death in 2 Timothy 1:9, 10. That, too, declares a distinctive element of God's wisdom, that though we are subject to death, the power of death over us here and now becomes inoperative. The same is true in regard to Satan's power in our lives, as declared in Hebrews 2:14. The words of 1 John 4:4 fit perfectly here: "Ye are of God, little children, and have overcome them: because greater is he [Christ] that is in you, than he that is in the world."

The Difference between Divine and Human Wisdom

The wisdom of God is immeasurably different from the wisdom of this age. Paul states this unequivocally in 1 Corinthians 2:6. It will pay us to examine in what way they differ, so that we may not waste time pursuing the wrong kind of wisdom.

In Luke 16:1–13, the Lord gives us a parable of a business manager who received notice from his wealthy employer that he was about to be dismissed. The manager thought of his bleak future without money and friends. So, before his dismissal, still acting as a business manager, he forgave in part the debts of two of his master's debtors. Thus he shrewdly took advantage of the little time left in his master's employ to make provision for the future by securing the friendship of two people who would be inclined to help if he were ever in need. Our Lord commended this man's action as wise, saying, "The children of this world are in their generation wiser than the children of light" (v. 8).

Interestingly enough, the phrase, "the children of this world," contains the same Greek word—*aiōnos,* "age"—as 1 Corinthians 2:6, "the wisdom of this age" and "the rulers of this age. "The wisdom of this business manager lay in his making provision for his material needs. That was an example of the wisdom of his generation or age. The Lord does not say he was in *all things* wiser than the ordinary Christian, but that the children of darkness are wiser in their own generation. That is all that can be said of them. Their wisdom is limited to the material world. It lacks balance; life is not a whole for them. They see only part of it, but they really develop that part.

As Alexander Maclaren says:

> If I am to call a man a wise man out and out, there are two things that I shall have to be satisfied about concerning him. The one is, what is he aiming at? and the other, how does he aim at it? In regard to the means, the men of the world . . . carry away the supremacy. Let in the thought of the end, and things change. Two questions reduce all the world's wisdom to stark, staring insanity. . . . "What are you doing it for?" . . . "And suppose you get it, what then?" Nothing that cannot pass the barrier of these two questions satisfactorily is other than madness, if taken to be the aim of a man's life. You have to look at the end, and the whole circumference of the circle of the human being, before you serve out the epithets of "wise" and "foolish."

It is foolish for one to think that they consist only of an aggregate of chemical substances that can be satisfied with material things. Yet that is what this age of sin considers wisdom. How wise his own generation would have considered the successful rich farmer of Luke 12:16–21. His warehouses were full, obviously as the result of human wisdom. But make no mistake; this was not the wisdom of God. The farmer in his moment of material affluence said, "Soul, thou hast much goods laid up for many years; take thine ease, eat, drink, and be merry" (v. 19). How foolish to think that one's soul can be satisfied with material things. The rich man had left out God as the only One who could satisfy his soul. The man who makes anything but God his end and aim may be relatively wise, but in the absolute sense he is foolish. Such people possess wisdom of a sort, as Paul recognized and our Lord acknowledged, but it is earthly wisdom, pertaining only to this age.

Take a sober look at yourself. You are an eternal being, and as such your aims should be of equal duration. An eternal man ought to make eternal things his aim; otherwise he is foolish, or only partially wise, in that he cares for only part of his life. Your treasures should last as long as you will, not only for this earth and age. "Their inward thought is, that their houses shall continue forever, and their dwelling places to all generations; they call their lands by their own names. . . . This their way is their folly" (Ps. 49:11, 13).

It is folly indeed to live for this age only, and to be governed by a wisdom that considers only the temporary. The wisdom of this age is inadequate to satisfy your spiritual needs, for as Paul says later in this second chapter of 1 Corinthians, you are a spirit as well as a body, and your spiritual need can only be satisfied by the Spirit of God. It is absurd for a man to fix his hopes and limit his aims and life-purposes within the bounds of what is destined to fade and perish. The fading and perishing are inherent in the phrases used by Paul in 1 Corinthians 2:6, "the wisdom of this age . . . the wisdom of the rulers of this age, them who perish." It is as if he were saying that this age, like its rulers, will pass away and be succeeded by others. But you will live on beyond this age. Therefore your philosophy of life must embrace that which is to come.

If you get involved in the mad race to accumulate things and leave God out, you will lose everything. Our Lord said, "What shall it profit a man, if he shall gain the whole world [*kosmos,* i.e., what this *aiōn,* 'age,' can offer], and lose his own soul?" (Mark 8:37). The closer to God we are, the more peace and happiness we shall experience. A baker never expects to get a better cake than the ingredients he puts into it. Yet many people who complain that life is not as rewarding as they expected it to be forget that in leaving out God they have left out that which alone can give life its glory, hope, love, and joy.

The wise man according to God not only sets his affections on the things that are above, but he also busies himself with specific and worthwhile tasks. Although we are not to have the wisdom of this age, which so often means each one for himself, we are to labor in the age in which God has placed us so that others may know that there is something beyond it. God expects us to work right where we are today. We are not to become so other-worldly that we forget that we belong to this age in fulfilling our responsibilities to God and our fellowmen. But neither are we to become so comfortable with this age that we adopt its philosophy.

We cannot shirk our responsibilities by saying that God gave others greater opportunities and gifts. In His plan, God designed each of us to fill a certain niche. If we fail Him, we will leave forever undone what He put us into the world to do. We might well emulate St. Francis, who while hoeing in his garden one day was asked, "If you knew that you were going to die tonight, what would you do?" "I would just keep on hoeing my garden," was his reply. Keep on hoeing that plot of ground God has given you, with an eye to its eternal value in His sight (Youngdahl 1955, 141–47).

LESSONS:

1. Any who doubt that the lives of men can be transformed by the power of God should go looking for them in the right places; he will be amazed.

2. Paul wanted the Corinthian Christians to realize that though their faith was not the product of human wisdom and reasoning, it did not lack real wisdom.

3. The basic thesis of Paul in 1 Corinthians is that, when man receives Christ, the power of God makes the natural fool, who mistakenly thinks himself wise, into a really wise person.

4. Not all Christians have the capacity to understand God equally; their understanding of Him is proportionate to their spiritual growth.

5. The closer we are to the heart of God, the clearer we hear His voice of wisdom; the more mature we become as Christians, the more God will reveal to us.

6. Human wisdom is changeable while divine wisdom is eternal. God's truth remains forever; that, therefore is what we should preach.

7. Men with "deceitful and desperately wicked" hearts cannot be changed by outward reformation, by any philosophy of man, or by any system of our times. Their basic need is inward cleansing.

8. Although the children of darkness really develop the wisdom of their own generation of the material world, their wisdom lacks balance. Life is not a whole for them.

9. The man who makes anything but God his end and aim may be relatively wise, but in the absolute sense he is foolish.

10. We are not to become so other-worldly that we forget that we belong to this age in fulfilling our responsibilities to God and our fellowmen, but neither are we to become so comfortable with this age that we adopt its philosophy.

1 Cor. 2:7 | *How to Enjoy God without Fully Understanding Him*

But we speak the wisdom of God in a mystery, even the hidden wisdom, which God ordained before the world unto our glory.

Why Are There Mysteries in Life?

Why does the apostle Paul declare in 1 Corinthians 2:7 that he speaks the wisdom of God "in a mystery"? Why is God's wisdom enveloped in mystery instead of clarity and simplicity? We know that nature itself is unfathomably mysterious. One scientist said that the most wonderful thing in the universe was that little filament of nerve we call "an ant's brain." By some secret that we cannot fathom, it holds ideas as subtle and complex as those upon which our highest civilization rests.

Look within yourself, and you will behold a mystery you cannot explain. There is a great deal of mystery in the world around us and inside of us. To this element of mystery both believer and unbeliever attest. Here is the testimony of a medical doctor:

> In an anatomy room a dead body meant nothing to me. I could not visualize the man or woman it might have been. Life left few records on the immobile face. For weeks I worked, and each day the wonder grew.
> Then one day I was working on an arm and hand, studying the perfect mechanical arrangements of the muscles and tendons, how the

sheaths of certain muscles are split to let tendons of certain muscles through, so that the hand may be delicate and small and yet powerful. I was all alone in the laboratory when the overwhelming belief came: a thing like this is not just a chance but a part of a plan, a plan so big that only God could have conceived it. Religion had been to me a matter of form, a thing without conviction, and now everything was an evidence of God—the tendons of the hand, the patterns of the little butterfly's wings—all was part of a purpose.

In creation the appearance of light did not drive away all darkness. Each day is succeeded by a night. The day is an opportunity, the night is a mystery. That there are mysteries in creation none but a fool can deny. A wise man recognizes the mysterious element in creation. But the apostle Paul wants us equally to recognize the mysterious element in revelation and in God's plan of redemption. God made the world for man. He then made man. That is creation. But man sinned and fell from favor and communion with his Creator. Therefore God had to recreate man, and the world in which God's recreated beings will ultimately dwell.

It is only reasonable, therefore, that as in creation there is an element of mystery, so there is also in the process and concept of redemption. It is of the redemption of man through the crucified Christ that Paul speaks to the Corinthians in the first two chapters of his first letter to them. Here in 1 Corinthians 2:7 he bursts out in a declaration we shall do well to ponder carefully. "But we speak the wisdom of God in a mystery." Although much about redemption is clear to us, not all of it is—and that for a purpose. The gospel is the wisdom of God, which means that God did not make a mistake; His wisdom is infallible. It is also the power of God. When God sets out to save a person, His power is irresistible. Wisdom and power, then, are the two main ingredients of the gospel. They are shrouded in mystery: how the gospel was conceived and how it is executed in each human life.

Men often claim that they would believe in God, they would accept Christ and His redemption, if it were all much clearer. They object to the mysteriousness of the gospel. How can a thinking man accept a religion so full of mysteries, of elements that seem to have no reasonable explanation? Let us see if we can fathom why God shrouded His wisdom in the mysterious element of the gospel.

The main reason God did not explain everything to man, I believe, was that we might never lose a sense of His greatness. In the first place, He did not create our minds equal to His. To make us realize this, He shrouded His revelation in mystery. How could we maintain our sense of the infinity of God if everything about Him could be known? He reveals as much to us as He made us capable of receiving, just as you would reveal to a child only as much as you know his little mind is capable of absorbing. The fact that you know so much more than he causes him to look up to and trust you. This is how God acts.

We know that God is an infinite being. He is another world in Himself, too high for our speculations and too great for our descriptions. How can such vast and mighty concepts be crowded into our small and finite understanding? Heaven really enters into us, as we must into it, by a very narrow passage.

Since we acknowledge a mysterious element in God's creation, why reject a mysterious element in His revelation? There is a far greater joy in accepting God's wisdom in mystery with regard to the gospel than in the joy and admiration we feel in the presence of the mysterious element in creation. How shall our limited faculties measure the lengths of His eternity, the breadth and expansions of His immensity, the heights of His prescience, and the depths of His decrees? And last of all, that unutterable, incomprehensible mystery of the two natures united into one person as in Christ and also in us after our new birth, and again of one and the same nature diffused into a triple personality in the Godhead. These are fundamentals of our Christian faith, and yet they are mysteries to us. They are mysteries because the condition of our nature is such that it renders us incapable of fully understanding them. They who reject the gospel because of its mystery cannot know any of its transforming power.

The gospel is also mysterious because of its spiritual and abstract nature. That is why it cannot be verified by our physical senses. God is a spirit. Can you form any concept of what that means? The angels are spirits. Can you form a true representation of what they really are? We are so bound by the limitations of our minds in the sphere of space and time that we find it difficult to conceive of anything beyond them.

Let me illustrate. Here is a man born blind. Can he, merely by hearing of them, conceive in his mind of all the varieties and properties of color? How foolish it would be for a blind man to conclude that because he cannot see colors they do not exist. He simply lacks the capacity for seeing them. And it would be equally foolish for us to reject the existence, the reality, of that which is mysterious to us and which has been revealed to us by God. As Paul says in 1 Corinthians 2:10, 11:

> But God hath revealed them [the elements of mystery in the gospel] unto us by his Spirit: for the Spirit searcheth all things, yea, the deep things of God. For what man knoweth the things of man, save the spirit of man which is in him? even so the things of God knoweth no man, but the Spirit of God.

Why Does God Keep So Many Secrets from Us?

The apostle Paul is not afraid to declare that the gospel is a mystery. In our previous study we saw that God's wisdom is shrouded in mystery because we are limited in comprehension, as well as the fact that much of it is beyond us due to its spiritual and abstract nature. But there is a third reason, as Paul tells us in 1 Corinthians 2:7. This is that God's actions in redemption are so strange and different from what our actions as humans would be.

What is redemption? It is the work of the Lord Jesus Christ, God the Son, becoming man in order to satisfy the Father's justice by dying on the cross for man's sin. To the natural man, this seems mysteriously unreasonable. Man expects the offender to take the initiative in seeking reconciliation and not the offended one. God did not need man to be reconciled to Him. Man was the one in need. It would have been an act of perfect justice if God, instead of dying for man, had utterly destroyed him as a result of his sin. Instead, we have a Father delivering up an innocent and infinitely beloved Son to be sacrificed for the redemption of His enemies whom He might justly abhor. And, on the other hand, we cannot fathom how a Son who loved His Father should lay down His life for the declared enemies of Him whom He so transcendently loved, and of Himself, too. Such a transaction is contrary to all human methods. Yes, God's wisdom is different from ours, "For my thoughts are not your thoughts, neither are your ways my ways, saith the Lord" (Is. 55:8). Nor is His nature like our nature or His Persons as our persons.

The mystery of the gospel is especially evident when we come to the conversion of a sinner, due to the change of man's sinful nature commonly called the work of regeneration or the new birth. Men rightfully wonder at the strange power and efficacy of that which enables a man to break loose from inveterate appetites and desires that are so violent and appear so early, and replace them with new ones of an entirely opposite nature. When the Lord told Nicodemus, a Jewish rabbi, that he must be born again, he was amazed, as if it were a great paradox and an impossibility. He immediately began to question "How can these things be?" (John 3:9). Yes, the new birth is God's wisdom in a mystery. Because it is a mystery, we need not keep silent about it but proclaim it.

Because of the mysteriousness of the gospel, you do not appropriate it through your mind but through your faith, your heart. Belief begins where knowledge stops; and since there is something beyond knowledge, as reason concludes there must be, it would be the height of stupidity to refuse to appropriate it. The means, however, must correspond to the end you want to reach. You cannot catch the sound waves all around you in the air with your bare hand; you need a radio receiver. And to catch the wisdom of God shrouded in mystery, you need faith that transcends knowledge. This is why faith is constantly stressed in the Scriptures as the means by which man appropriates God's mysterious gift of the new birth through Christ Jesus. Knowledge will not enable you to be born again. It must be by faith. Make no mistake, there is a perfect interaction between faith and knowledge. One succeeds the other as night succeeds day, and they both form part of a whole. So he who has received the mysterious gospel by faith does not walk in darkness but in the light, for faith is turned to knowledge as the wisdom of God is appropriated by the heart of man.

But you may say, "Would not it have been easier for us to receive the gospel had it not been so mysterious?" No, I do not believe so. The very wisdom of God is demonstrated in the mysteriousness of the Christian faith. Let us consider some of the reasons.

First of all, this mystery was wisely designed by God to produce awe, reverential fear, in men's minds. Ever since the first man rebelled against God, his descendants have been characterized by wanting to do their own thing, no matter what the consequences. But God meant man for a supernatural spiritual end: the adoration of the Creator and the glory of God. Therefore He had to devise some method to abridge and control his natural desires. This could only be done by imprinting apprehensions of dread and terror upon his judgment by nonplusing the world with certain new and unaccountable revelations of Himself and His divine methods. If it were not for the mysteriousness of God's wisdom in nature and redemption, man would be uncontrollable. The little fear and dread of God he has now would have diminished. It is the old story of familiarity breeding contempt. That is, what you can conquer you tend to disdain, and knowledge is a form of conquest over the thing or person you know. Distance preserves respect, and we still imagine some transcendent worth in things above our reach. Do you think that the Holy of Holies would have been so venerated by the Jews had they been permitted to enter it? Even the High Priest was permitted to enter only once a year. God in His wisdom ordained this because He knew that familiarity with holy things might insensibly lessen the reverential awe that sacred things were to maintain upon men's thoughts.

Another mystery devised by God's wisdom is that He withholds Himself from our physical sight. Many men in their absence have been greatly admired for their accomplishments but find a diminution of respect upon their personal presence. That is what happened in the case of the apostle Paul and the Corinthians. We read in 2 Corinthians 10:10, "For his letters, say they, are weighty and powerful, but his bodily presence is weak, and his speech is contemptible." He was more highly esteemed away from them than in their presence. For this reason kings usually do not mingle freely with their subjects, for a person seen often ceases to be admired or respected. Even the sun in all its glory is so commonplace a thing as to be taken for granted, while in an eclipse it commands the attention of everyone.

God has kept a great deal as a mystery in order to humble the pride of man's reason. The pride that caused man and certain angels to fall in the first place was founded on an inordinate desire for knowledge. Man wanted to be like God in knowledge, and so he fell. And now, if he wants to be like God in happiness, too, God will effect it in such a way as to convince man to his face that he knows nothing. The whole course of his salvation will be all riddle and mystery to him. Instead of evidence and clear knowledge, he must be contented with the dim light of faith, which guides only in the strength and light of another's knowledge, and is properly seeing with another's eyes. He is brought to the realization that apart from this dependence, faith is wholly unable to inform him about the great things of peace with God by any immediate inspection of those things themselves. Therefore, as the primitive effect of knowledge was first to puff up and then to throw down, so the contrary method of grace and faith is first to depress and then to lift up and advance.

God's wisdom is in mystery finally, to spur us on to search for what is not easily obtainable. No man studies those things that are self-evident. The foundation of all inquiry is the obscurity as well as the worth of the thing inquired after. The gospel hidden in mystery, therefore, should arouse our best and most active faculties. That is why we are commanded to search the Scriptures, not simply to read them. They are the great repositories of all the truths and mysteries of our faith. They are a rich mine that we shall do well to dig into and shall never exhaust. Just as gold and diamonds and most other precious stones and metals lie concealed in the depths of the earth, so the most valued things of revelation are concealed by the great Creator and Redeemer from the common view of the world. Only as this mystery stimulates us to dig into the Word shall we unearth the treasures that God has there for us (South 1855, 1:249–58).

Is It Reasonable to Reject the Gospel because It Is Mysterious?

"I do not understand, therefore I do not believe. I reject the gospel because it is full of mysteries." This is one of the favorite arguments of unbelief. And people expect us to believe their argument in this way is intelligent. The apostle Paul considered the mysterious element of the gospel as a help rather than a hindrance to man. That is why he did not try to hide the fact. He openly admits it in 1 Corinthians 2:7: "But we speak the wisdom of God in a mystery, even the hidden wisdom, which God ordained before the world unto our glory."

In this verse, Paul uses the same verb as in verse 6, *laloumen,* "we speak." It denotes declaration, without necessarily attempting to give a reason for what one says. Paul simply told forth the wisdom of God, that wisdom which originates with and belongs to God. The conjunction *alla,* "but," puts the wisdom of God in contrast to the wisdom of this age and its rulers mentioned in the previous verse. Paul is not afraid to declare that this wisdom of God goes beyond the natural comprehension of man. It is "in mystery," not to shame man but for his glory, for his good. Thus the mysteries in the gospel and in all Christianity are not something to hide, but to declare, and they should lead you to a saving faith; that will be glory for you. These mysteries should not hinder you but should help you to believe.

If you claim a right to understand everything in the Christian faith before you will believe it, you are claiming something that is first of all unjust. You are demanding of God that which He does not really owe you. God was free to give us a revelation or not, as He chose. He decided to do so. The next step was for Him to cause His revelation to be believed. He has chosen a variety of ways to accomplish this. He has provided us with historical evidence. The Bible is God's revelation to us. If history corroborates its truth, then we can accept His revelation.

Did the prophetic utterances of Scripture come true? A careful study proves that they did; and some people accept this as evidence of the truthfulness of the Bible. There are others who satisfy themselves with the internal evidence of the Scriptures.

In the Bible, they find the state of their souls perfectly described, their wants fully expressed, and the true remedies for their maladies completely indicated. Their hearts are moved, changed, renovated by the mysterious influence of these holy writings. They acquire a conviction of which they cannot always give an account to others, but which is none the less legitimate, irresistible, and immovable.

Thus God has given what He promised, sufficient evidence, external and internal, for us to acquire faith in His sufficiency to save all who come to Him through Christ. He has given enough to satisfy the need of your soul but not always the curiosity of your mind. God has proved Himself wise in allowing us to be in the dark as far as His mysteries are concerned so that He may protect us from harmful familiarity. God has come close to us in Jesus Christ so that He could save us from sin. But at the same time He wants to remain in our thoughts as the inconceivable God who reigns before all time, who includes in Himself all existences and all conditions of existence, the center of all thought, the Law of all law, the supreme and final reason of everything! So then, if you are just, instead of reproaching Him for the secrets of His revelation and His gospel, you will be grateful that He has enveloped you in mysteries.

In the second place, it is unreasonable to expect God to reveal everything to us. Would you not be unreasonable if you expected to hold the whole ocean in the hollow of your hand? What makes you think that you are wise in rejecting an omnipotent, eternal, infinite God and His wisdom because He does not fit into the limits of your intelligence! It would be utterly unreasonable if a finite being could embrace all there was in an infinite God and allow nothing beyond its grasp. It would be foolish for God to allow you to know everything and not to reserve anything to Himself. Then there would be nothing that you would learn and nothing that you would trust Him for.

As God has constituted this world, mysteries multiply with discoveries. God has been gracious in allowing us to make discoveries, and He has given us the capacity to receive revelations. But no learner in this world of ours can deny the fact that the more we discover, the more astonished we are at how much there is left to discover. Every bit of knowledge is succeeded by a realization of ignorance. The reality of the gospel is a well-attested fact. It is the highest possible expression of God's wisdom He has given us. But the higher a mountain, the greater the shadow it throws. Shall we reject the mountain because we stand in its shadow? That would be foolish. Let us rather be grateful for the shade it provides. As in the physical world we daily submit to a thousand things we do not understand, so let us do in the spiritual world, for both worlds have the same Creator. Our very existence is a mystery, yet we do not on that account reject it.

In the third place, to desire the knowledge of all mysteries is to desire what is utterly useless. What is the goal of the gospel? To regenerate and save us. But it does attain this end wholly by the things it reveals. "Though I . . . understand all mysteries," says Paul, "and have not charity, I am nothing" (1 Cor. 13:2). The mysteries are like a bottle that contains medicine. It is the medicine that cures you, not the bottle. Without even questioning it, you accept the fact that the medicine could not be presented to you without its container. You do not reject the medicine simply because you do not understand the composition of the bottle.

Thus each truth that saves is contained in a mystery which in itself has no power to save. The great work of atonement is necessarily attached to the incarnation of the Son of God, which is a mystery. Your sanctification is connected with the Holy Spirit, whose influence is a mystery. The deity of Christ finds its attestation in the miracles, which are mysteries. Everywhere the light is born from darkness, and darkness accompanies the light, even as in the natural world day and night succeed each other and yet form part of a whole. To reject the light of God's Word, which brings you peace and eternal life simply because it is delivered in a context of mystery that you cannot fully analyze, is utter absurdity (Vinet 1908, 173–188.)

When Is Ignorance a Good Thing?

The fact that there are mysterious elements in Christianity, things I cannot explain, does not make me any more ashamed to preach it than it did the apostle Paul. In fact, he openly declared that God's wisdom is inseparably connected with mysteries, things that the mind of man is unable to comprehend. "We speak God's wisdom in mystery," he says. And then he goes on to tell us that it was all planned that way by God Himself.

It is no accident that certain things about God's creation and revelation are a mystery to us. Everything God does or does not do has a purpose. He never simply allows things to happen but controls and plans everything. Sometimes He tells us why, more often He does not. The Greek word translated "hidden," in the phrase, "the hidden wisdom," in 1 Corinthians 2:7, is *apokekrummenēn*, which literally means "that has been hidden." God is the agent here. He purposely does not tell us all that He knows, especially in relation to our redemption and all that is involved in it, such as the incarnation of God in Christ, or how the three persons of the Godhead can be three yet one, or how the death of Christ and the blood He shed can cleanse an impure man and make him a saint. All these things God did and does, but how and why, He has purposely refused to tell us.

Paul goes on to tell us that the wisdom of God which He purposely hid from us was predestined by Him before the ages, for our glory. The phrase translated "before the world" is *pro tōn aiōnōn* in Greek, which literally means "before the ages." The definite article before *aiōnōn* indicates here the eons or epochs known to man. In other words, Paul takes us back before the creation of the world and says that before there was anything, there was God, who planned to keep certain matters of His wisdom and knowledge hidden from men, His creatures. He did not make this decision in the course of history, but planned it beforehand. God's decisions are not made on the spur of the moment as many of ours are. Everything is predetermined according to His absolute knowledge.

The word that the Authorized Version translates "ordained" in 1 Corinthians 2:7 is *proōrisen* in Greek, which means "foreordained or predestinated." The goal of this predestination is divine sonship through Jesus Christ. God is never said to have predestined anyone to be lost. But nobody is ever saved without God having known it before he was ever born. Otherwise He would not be God. His wisdom, as Paul tells us, was predestinated before all known ages. Paul also tells us why God did not reveal everything to us, but left some things shrouded in mystery. It was "unto our glory," he says. Now what does that mean?

In Proverbs 25:2 we find an interesting declaration that fully complements 1 Corinthians 2:7. It says, "It is the glory of God to conceal a thing." Taking these two verses together, we conclude that what is for the glory of God is also for the glory of the believer in Christ. Remember, of course, that it was believers to whom Paul wrote this epistle. The word for "glory" in Greek is *doxan*, from the verb *dokeō*, "to appear, to recognize." In the New Testament it means "divine honor, divine splendor, divine power." It is radiance that is easily recognized and that shows forth the character of the person who displays it. Thus, to glorify someone actually means to recognize him for what he is. To glorify God is to recognize and acknowledge Him for all that He is.

When a person becomes a believer in and through Christ, he becomes a Christ-bearer. The wisdom of God becomes his own wisdom. Therefore the glory of Christ becomes his own glory, and others can recognize that Christ dwells in him. Of course, the ultimate glory of the believer will be when he is finally clothed in his resurrection body, like the glorious body of Christ. But he shares in the glory of Christ from the moment he receives Him as Savior and Lord. Thus, as it is the glory of God to conceal a thing, so it is the glory of the believer to gaze at the mysteries of God and declare them. He should feel in no way humiliated because he does not know everything in spite of his special relationship with God. It is rather for his glory to trust God, who from before the foundation of the world decided as part of His wisdom to keep certain things to Himself.

This attitude of the believer, that the secrecy of God actually adds to his own radiance, rather than making him appear stupid, is not shared by the natural man. An unbeliever wants a God who will tell him everything. His reasoning is, "If I am to have faith in somebody, I expect him to confide in me. I can't commit myself to someone who keeps secrets from me." The natural man resents reserve, secrecy, isolation, almost as sharply as though they were moral transgressions. We have heard a great deal about man's demands that a government should hold no secrets from its citizens. And this attitude carries over in the natural man's demands of God. If we are going to be friends, he argues, He had better not keep any secrets from me. But the fact remains that God does keep many secrets, and it seems to me that there are some secrets that every good government ought to keep to itself for the good of its citizens. Responsibility demands a certain amount of reserve. God is certainly responsible, and He exercises authority. But He keeps secrets. These are both for His glory and the glory of those who have become His children through faith in Christ. But this is not understood by unbelievers, even as some unrealistic citizens do not concede the necessity of a certain amount of secrecy on the part of their government.

Sometimes men cultivate the habit of concealment so that they may circumvent opposition and accomplish their crafty aims more adroitly. This reflects an attitude of contempt for others. But God's reserve is always noble. It is always in favor of man. And the mystery of mysteries is that it is both for His glory and the believer's glory. There are reservations in the knowledge God has given us of His nature, purpose, and government, but these reservations always rest upon pure and holy motives. God keeps nothing back for our injury. He hides nothing simply to put up barriers to keep us away from Himself. No mystery is meant to alienate us from God, but to attach us in closer bonds. It is the glory of the Christian to trust God who knows more than he does. That is more glorious for him than if he knew all that God knows.

God's Self-Sufficiency and Man's God-Sufficiency

What a stupendous statement we find in Proverbs 25:2 and 1 Corinthians 2:7, that God is glorified by mystery and so is the believer. A superficial thinker might object to a statement such as that. Because of any such possible objection, we should elaborate the point, because it is important to clear God and the Christian believer from any accusation of irrationality. Let us see what these mysteries are in the divine nature and government that bear direct witness to the glory of God and in consequence to the glory of the believer.

God holds back many things from us of His own unapproachable majesty and perfection. The silence He maintains is a sign of His self-sufficiency. Men cultivate frank habits in their relations with each other to engage the sympathy, approval, and cooperation that may be necessary to them in doing the work of their lives. The desire for sympathy is a proof of our individual inadequacy to face the problems of life. A great deal of the motive force we need fully to effect our work is stored up in the hearts around us, and frankness on our part establishes the line of communication necessary for the transmission of this force.

How weak we are without those social bonds! We can only be kept up to our present levels by popular sympathy, the action and interaction of mind on mind. We are not the solitary masters of our fate we sometimes think ourselves to be. Our very trustfulness, our eagerness to find some ear for our most sacred secrets, the satisfaction we find in sharing our hopes and cares and wrongs with those who are about us, are so many pathetic signs of finite dependence and frailty.

However, you may ask, "Does not God ask us to confess our innermost secrets to Him and to enter into sympathy and cooperation with Himself and His work?" Yes, He does, but for an entirely different reason from that of any of our fellow human beings. He actually does not need our help, and by the deliberate reserve of His revelations He asserts the separateness and sufficiency of His own mighty power. God can do all, if He chooses to, without the cooperation of a single finite being. He is the great Atlas who takes upon His own solitary nature all the work of a universe measureless to us in either time or space, without stooping to the task or straining a single faculty in the effort.

If He employs us at all, it is for our good and not because of His need. It is by a wonderful exhibition of graciousness that He calls our labor a service to Himself, but He is not dependent upon our help for the fulfillment of His designs. He permits and indeed invites that help, but His power is separate, sufficient, solitary. Isaiah 40:14 asks, "With whom took he counsel, and who instructed him, and taught him in the path of judgment, and taught him knowledge, and showed to him the way of understanding?" The answer, of course, is "No one."

Does God interpret at once every providential enigma in your life? He needs only the cooperation of your life, and not necessarily of your understanding also, that He may bring to benign fruitfulness all the unknown issues with which your life is fraught. God can do His work without help. He does not need to debate its principles with you or me. His secrets symbolize a high authority that can never be transferred to another. In His revelations there are majestic and solemnizing reserves that demand our reverence. There can never be a greater glory for any believer than such reverence and confidence in God in the face of the mystery of His actions.

When Amy Carmichael went to India in 1895, she did not realize that for fifty-five years India would be her home and the children of India her beloved family. Nor did she know then that many beautiful, intelligent little girls in India were taken from their homes and trained to become temple women to satisfy the lusts of men in the degrading worship of Hindu gods. She first learned of the horrible custom in 1901 when a seven-year-old girl who had escaped from the temple was brought to her house. "What she told me darkened the sunlight," said Amy Carmichael. From that day the Lord laid upon her heart the burden of saving these girls from moral ruin and training them to do the will of the heavenly Father.

In 1931, Miss Carmichael slipped into a pit, broke her leg and dislocated her ankle. For nearly twenty years she was an invalid and rarely left her room. On the morning of the accident she had prayed, "Do anything, Lord, that will fit me to serve Thee and help these beloved children." In her confinement she wrote thirteen books that have blessed sufferers throughout the world.

Why should any child of God suddenly become an invalid? That is a mystery. God does not choose to reveal the reason, except as it may become apparent in retrospect. But it is always for

His glory, for "It is the glory of God to conceal a thing" (Prov. 25:2); and "the wisdom of God in a mystery" (1 Cor. 2:7), which He has hidden from the creation of the world, is also for the glory of the believer. The believer being a child of God is glorified whenever his Father is glorified, even as in our human families the glory of a father is automatically the glory of the son. It is a glorious thing for man, whenever mysterious circumstances arise in his life, to be God-sufficient and not to seek human explanations for God's actions in his life. The glory of the believer is absolute trust and confidence. It is a glorious thing to know that God, whose very own you are, makes no mistakes in directing or permitting those things that cross the path of your life. As A. M. Overton expresses it in a beautiful poem:

> My Father's way may twist and turn,
>   My heart may throb and ache,
> But in my soul I'm glad I know
>   He maketh no mistake.
> My cherished plans may go astray,
>   My hopes may fade away,
> But still I'll trust my Lord to lead,
>   For He doth know the way.
> Though night be dark and it may seem
>   That day will never break,
> I'll pin my faith, my all in Him,
>   He maketh no mistake.

And the greatest glory for any man is to trust God so much that no matter in what circumstances he finds himself, he realizes that it cannot be because God has made a mistake but that it is part of His eternal plan that is wise, mysterious, and has an eternal purpose for the glory of the believer.

Why Should Believers Welcome Mysteries?

Our character could not become what God desires it to be if it were not for the mysteries with which He surrounds us. For that reason, mysteries are beneficial. They glorify God and the believer, for they provide the discipline and exaltation that our character needs.

If our life bears God's image, whatever brings elements of moral splendor, strength, and refinement into it must reflect new honor upon the name of God. The veiled truth sometimes calls out a higher faith, a more chastened submission, a more childlike obedience in God's people than the truth that is unveiled. Such an end sufficiently justifies God's silence and reservation upon questions that we are restless to have settled.

God conceals many things so that He may be magnified through His people's trust in the midst of darkness and uncertainty. On the other hand, it is just as true that mystery alone could never excite our faith. No genuine spirit of trust can spring up in ignorance. In God's dealings with us, the hidden and the revealed, the mystery and the defined truth, alternate with each other. The questions with which the universe challenges our thought divide themselves into two categories, as set forth in Deuteronomy 29:29: "The secret things belong unto the Lord our God, but those things which are revealed belong unto us and to our children." He creates and stimulates our trust. By what He chooses not to reveal He tests and braces and approves it. When our trust stands the strain of all the great mysteries that are about us, God is glorified, and His honor is seen to have been linked with the very secrecy of His providence.

All curiosity implies more or less of skepticism and mental uneasiness. If our faith were unlimited, we should not seek the answers to so many questions. Imagine a physician whose fidelity and skill have inspired such confidence that, when he is called in, no one ever dreams of asking what treatment he is adopting or of surreptitiously checking his diagnosis; or a commander to whom his chief gives a free hand, without asking him to divulge his plan of campaign. The man is not yet born who commands that kind of unlimited confidence. But God demands and deserves this matchless honor. He ordains not a few of the mysteries that confront us so that we may possess occasions for glorifying Him after this high fashion.

It is said that, when Michelangelo had become blind and feeble with age, he was led morning by morning into the Vatican museum that he might delight his artistic sense by passing his hand over the wonderful lines of the Torso. It was this deprivation of sight that possibly brought his guide, some lowly citizen, into touch with the master-hand, whose ability had put the stamp of a priceless value on many a canvas and marble.

In the same manner many problems are unexplained in the life of the believer so that God may come into closer touch with us and be our guide in the solemn darkness. That is glory for both God and us. We grope, as He helps and sustains us, at the outline of wonderful mysteries that lie about us. Here it is the Infinite who guides the finite, and yet He feels more honored by the fact that we hang upon His help than the lowly Roman citizen by the touch of the great Michelangelo's trembling hand. "It is the glory of God to conceal a thing," because by the very shadows in which He hides it we are cast with greater dependence upon His sympathy and care, and come into truer and more childlike contact with His Spirit.

God conceals many things so that He may protect us from needless pain and fear and magnify His own gentleness. We are so timid and tender and unschooled that God often has to place the shadow of His hand across our vision, just as the Alpine guide will blindfold a nervous traveler so that he may guide him unharmed across some terrific chasm. Do not think you are strong enough to peer undismayed into all the deep mysteries of eternity. God has hidden much from you in tender care for your peace and well-being as well as to magnify His own gentleness.

God conceals some things from us to excite us to nobler and more strenuous endeavor in our search after truth. Some truths we must know at once, for they are necessary to our very lives. Those are the truths that are the subject of common revelation. On the other hand, among the things that are not revealed there may be truths that we shall come to know through our thought and struggle and deepening spirituality of life, temporary mysteries that it is best for us to know through conflict, experience, sustained contemplation. We benefit a great deal in our struggle to unlock the secrets of earth; how much more in our endeavor to unlock the secrets of heaven that are meant to be unlocked through spiritual endeavor?

There is no doubt that there is special divine favor of God for His children . One evidence of this is the capacity He gives them to receive His wisdom in mystery so that they may be partakers of His glory. God's wisdom in mystery is meant to honor His own chosen servants. The greatest proof that a sovereign can give of his favor to a subject is to entrust him with some high State secret. "It is given unto you to know the mysteries of the kingdom of heaven, but to them it is not given" (Matt. 13:11). God withholds many things from common knowledge so that He may entrust them to those in whom He delights. Abraham was a child of God; therefore God entrusted him with special knowledge. We read in Genesis 18:17, "Shall I hide from Abraham that thing which I do?" "The secret of the Lord is with them that fear him; and he will shew them his covenant" (Ps. 25:14).

The things that are open to the understanding of God's servants are often veiled from those who have "no fear of God before their eyes" (Rom. 3:18). Said the disciples, "Lord, how is it that thou wilt manifest thyself unto us, and not unto the world?" (John 14:22). The answer is that they love the Lord, and such love is the foundation of a fellowship to which the world must be ever strange. If every deep thing were fathomed by the man who is self-exiled from God, the special privilege of those who live in close friendship with God would be lost. His people are honored and glorified by admission to His deep and hidden counsels, and in their honor and glory He Himself is exalted. Therefore welcome mysteries, since they mean God's glory and ours as believers (see Selby 1889, 49–70).

LESSONS:

1. He who has received the mysterious gospel by faith does not walk in darkness but in the light, for faith is turned to knowledge as the wisdom of God is appropriated by the heart of man.

2. God has kept a great deal as a mystery in order to humble the pride of man's reason.

3. God's wisdom is in mystery to spur us on to search for that which is not easily obtainable.

4. The mysteries in the gospel and in all Christianity are not something to hide but to declare, and they should lead to saving faith.

5. The secrecy of God adds to the radiance of the believer.

6. The greatest glory for any man is to trust God so much that no matter in what circumstances he finds himself, he realizes that it cannot be because God has made a mistake, but that it is part of His eternal plan.

1 Cor. 2:8 | *What Knowledge Cannot Achieve*

Which none of the princes of this world knew: for had they known it, they would not have crucified the Lord of glory.

Religious Rulers Reject the Messiah out of Ignorance

The crucifixion of Christ is the greatest evidence of the stupidity of natural man. I hope that statement startles you enough to ask why. In 1 Corinthians 2:8, Paul speaks of the wisdom of God in a mystery, "Which none of the princes of this world knew: for had they known it, they would not have crucified the Lord of glory." Not a single ruler of this world knew this wisdom of God. That is some statement. They may have possessed a great deal of human wisdom, which was much admired by the people they ruled over, but there was not one of them who was characterized by the wisdom of God. Having never accepted God's revelation in Christ as the God-Man, they had consequently remained ignorant of God's wisdom.

Paul refers to the Jewish and Roman political leaders here, but in his time the former were also the ecclesiastical rulers. It was in the Sanhedrin that the first decision was taken to put Christ to death. These people had the Old Testament revelation to give them knowledge of the Messiah, but they rejected it. The truth about Christ almost got through to Pilate, but through cowardice he participated in the sentencing of Christ. He said, "I find in him no fault at all" (John 18:38).

While Christ was hanging on the cross, He testified to the ignorance of the people who were crucifying Him by saying, "Father, forgive them; for they know not what they do" (Luke 23:34). To his fellow Jews, Peter said, "And now, brethren, I know that through ignorance ye did it [crucified Christ], as did also your rulers [*archontes,* the same Greek word as in 1 Cor. 2:8]" (Acts 3:17). All these were ignorant of God's wisdom in sending Christ to the world; therefore, they crucified Him. They did not realize they were crucifying the only hope of their salvation and the personification of God's wisdom.

The trouble with the rulers who crucified Christ was that they tried to use their finite minds to comprehend the wisdom of infinity. This is an impossibility, just as it is impossible for an idea to be contained in a glass jar. They are incongruous. Infinity requires infinity to comprehend it. The verb that Paul uses for "knowing" here is *egnōken;* not a single one of the rulers of this age "did know," for if they "had known," *egnōsan,* they would not have crucified Christ.

Man Receives the Messiah by Faith, Not Human Knowledge

Both words come from the verb *ginōskō,* which means knowledge that man acquires through his own natural mind as a result of his own experience and investigation. It refers to man's effort to reach up to God. Is he able to? No, for God is so high and man so low that this is a sheer impossibility. Therefore, instead of accepting that which God sent from heaven, His Son, some of these people who through their own knowledge could not reach up to God gave up, saying that there was nothing beyond their reach. But they did something infinitely worse. They killed that which God had sent from heaven.

The meaning of the word *ginōskō*, "know," in this context goes beyond mere intellectual knowledge. It also means to appropriate as truth, as reality for one's own life. It is the same word as in John 8:32, "And ye shall know [*gnōsesthe*] the truth, and the truth shall make you free."

A fascinating verse in the Greek text is John 8:55, "Yet ye have not known him [God the Father]; but I know him; and if I should say, I know him not, I shall be a liar like unto you: but I know him, and keep his saying." Here two distinct Greek words are translated by the same English word "know." In the Greek, the first "know" ("ye have not known him," referring to the Jews who were discussing with the Lord Jesus) is *egnōkate*, from *ginōskō* or *gignōskō*, which means to know by human endeavor and experience. Ye did not know God. You could not reach up to Him. But all other "know's" in this verse are the Greek verb *oida*, to know intuitively as part and parcel of one's nature. Christ was asserting that He knew God because He was of the same nature as God the Father. We believers know God as a result of our acceptance of the Lord Jesus Christ, having thus become the children of God. Having acquired the nature of God, we intuitively know God, His wisdom in mystery. In fact, accepting the crucified Christ is accepting the greatest mystery that God ever revealed to man. We do not reach up through the help of our human knowledge, but we receive that which has come down from heaven. Those who reach up, and cannot reach high enough, decide to kill God's heaven-sent gift, but those who accept it by faith are transformed by it into God's image and therefore do not simply *ginōskein*, know experientially, but *eidenai*, know intuitively.

The wisdom of God in a mystery, the culmination of which is Christ on the cross of Calvary, cannot be acquired by the process of human thinking but must be received. It is too deep for any to see with his unaided intellect. May I ask you carefully to read Job 28. You will see there a knowledge of natural things, but wisdom as a gift of God. In verse 12 we find a question: "But where shall wisdom be found? and where is the place of understanding?" Scholars believe that verses 7 and 8 should follow verse 12. "There is a path which no fowl knoweth, and which the vulture's eye hath not seen: the lion's whelps have not trodden it, nor the fierce lion passed by it."

In other words, there is something in the depth of the earth that neither the ruler of the air (the eagle), nor the ruler of the forest (the lion), can see and appropriate. Job is thinking of the miner's track under the earth. There are treasures there, yet they are beyond the sight and reach of the mighty on top of the earth. This is a humbling reminder that there may be more things happening round about us than we can see either with microscope or telescope. We must not make the fact that we cannot see or explain these things a reason to deny their reality and worth because by so doing we may be shutting ourselves off from an entire realm.

The cross of Christ is something you cannot possibly fathom with human understanding, but it is what you need most to satisfy your soul. Therefore, stop reaching to grasp the meaning of life, and receive Him who has come down, the Lord of glory. That will indeed be your greatest glory, glory that no attainment of knowledge can give you (see Alexander 1930, 117:87–88).

LESSONS:

1. The trouble with the rulers who crucified Christ was that they tried to use their finite minds to comprehend the wisdom of infinity.

2. In fact, accepting the crucified Christ is accepting the greatest mystery that God ever revealed to man.

3. The wisdom of God in a mystery, the culmination of which is Christ on the cross of Calvary, cannot be acquired by the process of human thinking, but must be received.

1 Cor. 2:9

How You Can Know God's Inner Secrets

But as it is written, Eye hath not seen, nor ear heard, neither have entered into the heart of man, the things which God hath prepared for them that love him.

You May Not Be Able to Understand It, Yet It Can Make You Happy

Many of the cultured men of Corinth had weighed the apostle Paul's message in their intellectual scales and rejected it as worthless. That a crucified Jew should be the Son of God, the Redeemer of the world, and the final Judge of all men, seemed to them the delusion of ignorant and crazy minds.

Previously, in 1 Corinthians 2:6–8, Paul had declined to submit the mysteries of God to their handling. His wisdom is beyond you, he declared, and this is why you cannot explain it. It is full of mysteries, but that is the glory of it, and the glory of those who have accepted it in and through Christ.

Then he gave them something recalled from Isaiah 64:4, not an exact quotation but something that he believed paralleled it in the situation he was facing. Isaiah said, "For since the beginning of the world men have not heard, nor perceived by the ear, neither hath the eye seen, O God, beside thee, what he hath prepared for him that waiteth for him." The calamities of Israel were great. The Israelites were being assured that the compensation of God must be equally as great. The words accompany the passionate cry to God for interference in the world's affairs: "Oh that thou wouldest rend the heavens, that thou wouldest come down" (Is. 64:1). Paul refers to God's interference in the affairs of men in sending His Son to die for their salvation. This was rejected by the unbelieving Corinthians as nonsense.

In Isaiah we see the marvelous God who works for them that wait for Him. He is not marvelous to everybody. There is a condition. In faith you have to wait for Him. The parallel in 1 Corinthians 2:9 is the God-Man Jesus Christ, who becomes the wisdom of God and the power of God unto salvation, not for everybody but only for those who love Him. And they can only love Him if they have received Him as their Savior from sin (Morgan 1955, 9:316–27).

The gospel of the Lord Jesus Christ, and the redemption He purchased for us on the cross, as well as His power to transform lives, are not judged by the sight of the eyes and by the hearing of the ear, nor even by the trained and well-balanced intellect. The intellectuals called Paul a fool for believing the gospel. But he throws the ball back to them in this 9th verse of 1 Corinthians 2 by telling them that, if they were as smart as they thought they were, they would know better than to compare physical things with spiritual. The eye? the ear, the heart (that is, the senses), have their appointed capabilities, but do not expect them to do what they are not designed to do. The unbelieving Corinthians threw impolite words at Paul, such as "foolishness," to describe their view of the gospel he proclaimed, but he threw incontrovertible arguments back at them.

His argument here is that we as men belong to two worlds, the physical and the spiritual, the seen and the unseen, the temporal and the eternal—indissolubly united and unceasingly affecting one another. We may fill our lives with pleasure, work, and distractions that leave no time for reflection, but nonetheless we are subject, though it may be against our will, to forces of an invisible order. Or we may fix our eyes on a far-off heaven, and seek to shut out any thoughts of the mundane. Nevertheless, we shall find that we cannot escape from the present. We shall be constrained to confess that we cannot fully realize the glory of the Unseen except as it is reflected from the things of earth; and it is only as we use earthly things that we become capable of seeing the eternal things that they signify.

Thus the conviction is forced on us by actual experience that we belong to two worlds. Sooner or later in life, as the shadows of tribulation fall upon us and as death approaches, we conclude that life is born of darkness and dies in darkness. But more than this, we come to know that darkness, like the inimitable starlit spaces of the sky, reveals to us depths of God which we could not otherwise comprehend. We must be careful lest we give substance to the unseen by crowding into it things which eye hath seen or heard (see Westcott n.d., 12:89–94).

However, let us not make the mistake of thinking that Paul is speaking only of the future in this verse. He speaks of the unseen present and future. Heaven's glories begin on earth for the believer. The unseen which is our future is prepared by the present. It is an absolute perversion of Christianity to say that it is a "pie in the sky" religion. The sense of the Eternal in the present gives to things transitory a power of meaning for the believer that they cannot otherwise have. Christ makes the difference down here and up there.

> Heaven above is softer blue,
>   Earth beneath is sweeter green,
> Something lives in every hue
>   Christless eyes have never seen.
> Birds with sweeter songs o'erflow,
>   Flowers with newer beauty shine

> Since I know as now I know
> I am His and He is mine!
> —Author Unknown

Do not ever make the mistake of thinking that a Christian must look forward to having all his joys in heaven. Believers have every reason to be the happiest people on earth. A stranger in St. Louis stopped a policeman one Sunday morning and asked him to recommend a church. He directed him to one at a little distance. "What is the matter with these other churches that I see along the way?" asked the stranger. "Why don't you recommend them?" "To tell the truth," replied the policeman, "I am an unbeliever myself, but people coming out of that church are always happy. They are different. If I ever decided to go to church, that is where I would go. They've got something there that makes them happy." That something was the gospel of Jesus Christ. You may not be able fully to understand it, but it has the power to give you the joy, peace, and satisfaction of heart that the whole world cannot give you.

How Does Christianity Differ from Other Religions?

Every born-again believer in Christ has within him something that is hidden from the view of the unbeliever. Eye cannot see it. Ear cannot hear it. The mind of man cannot comprehend it. It is a mystery. But it is there. It is the redeeming grace of the Lord Jesus Christ in the lives of those who love God.

No one has expressed it better than John Bunyan. He wrote:

> The happy man was born in the city of Regeneration, in the parish of Repentance unto Life. He was educated in the School of Obedience, he works at the trade of Diligence and does many jobs of self-denial. He owns a large estate in the country of Christian Contentment and wears the plain garments of humility. He breakfasts every morning on spiritual prayer and sups every evening on the same. He also has 'meat to eat that the world knows not of.' He has gospel submission in his conduct, due order in his affection, sound peace in his conscience, sanctifying love in

his soul, real divinity in his breast, true humility in his heart, the Redeemer's yoke on his neck, the world under his feet, and a crown of glory over his head. In order to obtain this, he prays fervently, works abundantly, redeems his time, guards his sense, loves Christ, and longs for glory.

In 1 Corinthians 2:9 Paul does not enumerate the "things which God hath prepared for them that love him." Actually, this verse begins with the relative pronoun *ha*, "which," and translators had to add the word "things." In fact, the three words, "the things which," were all needed to express the Greek *ha*, "which." This word does not refer to persons but to something of neuter gender. We must not understand this to mean, however, just things without life and power. It stands for the experiences of the spiritual self of man that are beyond the comprehension of the physical senses. Paul is not speaking primarily of material things to be had in heaven as for instance the Mohammedans envision them. He is speaking principally of the experience of redemption through Christ. In the opening verses of this chapter Paul made specific allusion to the atoning work of Christ the crucified. He declared that he was determined to know nothing among men save Jesus Christ and Him crucified. This is the most important experience of life.

Of course, his cultivated hearers in the Greek world could not understand his exaltation of the cross as a pledge of eternal life, for to them it was a symbol of the deepest degradation. The apostle's reply to this was, You may object as you please to what I proclaim to be a fact—that Christ died for the unjust—but your objections weigh nothing with me, for I deliver the message as I received it from heaven itself. It is not a fantasy that I spun out of my own brain. It is not a system of faith I received from any school of men. It is not a thing that occurred to a human mind at all. I must declare the message as it was delivered to me. This

doctrine is not of men but of God. In many ways it is opposed
to men's conclusions, tastes, and prejudices.

What Paul wanted to emphasize was the fundamental dif-
ference between the gospel and all other religious systems.
Christianity is not just another religious system. It stands apart.
It is distinguished by the atonement accomplished by the Lord
Jesus Christ on the cross.

The idea of atonement itself is not new with Christianity.
You find it expressed in practically every system under heaven
the world over, and through all history. But when you observe
the wide difference between the human conception of atonement
and the gospel conception, the human may be summed up in one
sentence: Man so feared God that he offered his dearest and best
if thereby he might turn away God's anger. The gospel or Christian conception, on the other hand, may be summed up in the
most marvelous words that ever fell on mortal ears: "God so
loved the world that he gave his only begotten Son" (John 3:16).

You see the difference. In the human conception, man seeks
by his suffering, his sacrifice and blood, to reconcile God to himself. The difficulty, he thinks, is on God's side, not man's, and his
aim is to conciliate the heart of the Eternal. According to the
Christian concept, God by the suffering and blood of His only
begotten Son reconciled man to himself. The difficulty is not
upon God's side but upon man's. In the human idea, man is the
sufferer, God the recipient. In the gospel or Christian conception, God the Son is the sufferer, man the recipient. In the gospel
or Christian idea, God makes atonement. The one atonement
springs out of man's dread of God, and the other out of God's
love for man. So these two ideas are as far apart as the poles, and
can never by any ingenuity of human explanation be brought together or placed in the same class of thought.

What a wonderful thing this is, that the eternal God, the
Maker of heaven and earth, should at infinite cost to Himself

take away whatever barrier lay between this world and life eternal! That thought of God taking the sin of this world upon Himself never entered the heart of man outside the New Testament—never. Remember, you owe that tender conception to the gospel of Jesus Christ, beginning, end, and all together. Nowhere outside the New Testament is there even a hint of a God who so loved as to give Himself that man might be forgiven. The prevalent note in all other religious systems is salvation by human merit. But not in Christianity. Salvation is through the sacrifice of Christ. We can be saved, not because of what we have done, but because of what He has done for us, even when we were in enmity with Him. Consequently, if you take Christ out of Christianity, you have nothing left. Christianity is Christ. Without the cross, no human redemption exists. And the most wonderful part of the gospel is that it makes Christ your personal Redeemer and Lord (see Hanson 1911, 80:150–52.)

The Folly of Believing Only What Your Eyes Can See

You can know things in three ways: by personal observation, by way of instruction from others, and by way of pure reasoning. The apostle called these three ways of learning the "eye," the "ear," and the "heart." These give us an understanding of natural things, but not of the supernatural and eternal.

It is a great blessing to be able to see. Just imagine how ignorant we would be of all that is around us if we had never been able to see. How circumscribed is the world of the blind! And yet, marvelous as our natural vision is, our eyes cannot look upon the Creator of the world, cannot discover anything about the character of God. The eye is a physical organ, and it relates us to the physical world around us; whereas God is Spirit, and the salvation He offers through Christ is a spiritual salvation.

"Eye hath not seen," says Paul. The Greek verb used for "saw" (translated "hath seen" in the Authorized Version) is *eiden*, which in this context refers primarily to physical sight with the added sense of mental perception. A physical organ, the eye, has not physically seen those experiences which God has prepared for those who love Him. And this verb *eiden*, "saw," is in the second aorist, which means at any time in the history of the world.

But what about the crucifixion of the Lord Jesus Christ? Was that not a real physical event? Was it not visible to all the people who actually crucified Him and to all who watched it? It was a historical event that took place at a particular time in history. Many indeed saw Jesus crucified. Many heard Him speak from the cross. This is undeniable. God indeed prepared that event and many saw it with their own eyes. But they did not see the deeper implications of what that physical event represented—the redemption of the human race. They could not see how in and through that physical event a spiritual transformation of their being could take place. That had to be revealed to them by the Spirit of God. In order that you may see spiritual power and significance in a physical event, you must have spiritual discernment. You cannot see the possibility of conversion in the cross of Christ unless you allow the God who planned it all to enter your being and give you spiritual vision.

Paul is trying to teach here that there is a spiritual faculty available to men which can make them wiser in the things of the spirit than all that the wisdom of this world knows. And the merest child in faith may feel and know what the unconverted intellectual giant has no perception of. There are perceptions that no training can give, that no school can create: they are the gift of God, and these perceptions are often in the possession of the child, or the untutored woman, and even of the uneducated preacher, while the most omnivorous bookworm may be destitute of them. All through the first and second chapters of his first epistle to the Corinthians, Paul is teaching that there is such a thing as the foolishness of the learned and the wisdom of the unlearned.

Peter and John stood before the Jewish judges to be tried for healing a lame man. They had done what their learned judges could not do, by the power of the Christ whom their judges had crucified. These apostles had the power to tell the lame man, "Rise up and walk." That is power. The lame man could not see that power in Peter and John, although it was there. Eye could not see it, when it was released, but the lame man felt it. He rose and walked. But do you think that those judges could see that which was hidden in the apostles? "Now when they saw the boldness of Peter and John, and perceived that they were unlearned and ignorant men, they marvelled" (Acts 4:13). This miracle was performed through the power of Christ, a power that cannot be seen but that can be felt. Against their desires, the judges released the apostles, wondering why they, as learned men, should be influenced by men of such untrained intellects.

The Christian eye is the most discerning of all. It does not support natural ignorance, ignorance of the physical world. After all, who can deny that Christianity has been the leader in founding schools and colleges? But Christians, while not encouraging ignorance, recognize what the world often overlooks—that learning, in itself, has serious limitations. Misapplied learning is of little value, and often of great harm. And no amount of learning can save your soul from the guilt of sin.

Let me take you now to see Paul before King Agrippa, or Festus, or Felix. He flings out, in the face of all their splendor, his proud, pathetic challenge: "I would to God, that not only thou, but also all that hear me this day, were . . . altogether such as I am, except these bonds" (Acts 26:29). This saying, in its very tenderness, expresses the utmost contempt for all that these men enjoyed and were living for. Life for them meant sensual pleasures, pompous shows, command of money, power, and ambition—cups most of which Paul had tasted. He knew the quality of them, the measure of satisfaction they would yield. And he had stepped up from this to a higher platform, to a life in which vulgar ambitions were forgotten, and the pleasures of the senses pushed out by mightier joys; to a life in which enthusiasm, hope, love, great aims, the friendship of God, and fellowship with Christ, were supreme.

Standing there, with the chains upon his wrist, despised or pitied by all the spectators, he felt a joyous liberty, a serene calm, a fullness of unutterable emotion, a lofty grandeur of soul, such as he knew that they had never felt and known. He was quite sure that life meant more and deeper and nobler things to him than had ever entered their hearts to conceive. There had been revealed to him things which "eye hath not seen."

And it is always thus with souls to whom God has spoken His deeper things. The joy that they have is so refined and pure that they can look down upon lower joys with solemn and pathetic contempt. If you do not at times feel something of this, it is questionable whether you have any real spiritual feeling at all. As a Christian, you must have moments when you realize that the things which are dearest to you, and of infinitely greater importance than material blessings, are those experiences, hopes, emotions, and communications that belong to you as children of God, which are the gift of Christ to you, and which are no more understood by the unbelieving world than the pleasures of the intellect are understood by the man who cannot read or spell. If the best part of your lives is not hidden from the world, then it may be that you have no Christian life at all (see Anderson 1922, 89–95; Greenhough n.d., 78–82).

What Tradition and Reason Cannot Do for You

Two men were sent to check a rumor that iron lay beneath the surface of a certain piece of ground. One, a scientist and mineralogist, conscious of his own limitations, took along some instruments. The other, a buoyant, self-confident individual, said, "I believe what I can see; and what I cannot see I will not believe." He walked rapidly over the field and said, "Iron? Nonsense! I see no iron; there is no iron here." And that is what he stated in his report. The other man did not trust his eye at all, but looked at his instruments. The needle on one pointed to the fact that a rich deposit of iron did lie beneath the earth's surface. As he made his report he said, "My eyes could not see it, but my magnet discerned it."

As the eye cannot see minerals hidden in the earth, so it cannot see what is in the heart of God toward man. It can look upon the crucified Christ and fail to see God's plan of redemption. The eye stands for knowledge by personal observation. The Lord Jesus walked the streets of Palestine, but how many could really understand who He was and what He came to do? There was no outward beauty in Him that they should desire Him. The eye could not see what God had prepared in Him and through Him for the world.

"Nor ear heard . . . the things which God hath prepared for them that love him." The ear stands for knowledge acquired by listening to others. Paul is not suggesting that we need not speak of God's revelation to others in thus declaring the inability of our sense of hearing to reveal the secrets of God to us. Paul spoke of it. But he means that no amount of speaking about God and His salvation can possibly persuade a human being to accept it. There must be an element other than speaking and hearing, and that is the convicting power of the Holy Spirit enabling a man to appropriate the power of God unto salvation.

It is simply impossible for the secrets of the Christian life to be revealed to those who have no Christian beliefs and sentiments. People say to us, "Your joys are imaginary, your perceptions of God are self-delusions, your assurances and hopes and peace of mind and consciousness of forgiveness are your own creations. They are things that we do not feel, and do not understand, and do not believe."

Precisely! It would be a wonderful thing, indeed, if they did understand what they have never felt. You cannot make a deaf man understand music, though you spend years in instructing him. Nobody but a mother can quite understand what a mother's love for a child is. You might read all the volumes that treat of that affection, and ransack the whole dictionary of love, without being much wiser as to the real mystery of it. The only way to find that out is to become a mother. And the only way to discover the joy of divine forgiveness is to be forgiven.

Plato drew a picture of the worshipers in the old pagan Mysteries. They are going through the sacred dance to the sound of music in their midst. But spectators on a distant hillside who see their movements of joy, but cannot hear the music, conclude that these dancers are mad. Is that not akin to what the spectators said about the disciples at Pentecost—that they were drunk, full of new wine? Their joy was incomprehensible.

People outside the Christian faith are like these spectators. They cannot hear the music, and all the rest seems strange and inexplicable. They do not know the raptures that are felt when the load of sin is removed; when God, who has seemed far off, comes as near as a familiar friend; when life moves in heavenly places, overshadowed by the love of Jesus, and there is singing in the heart sweeter than all earthly music. They cannot know. They must taste before they can understand the things which God has revealed to them that love Him.

The third avenue of knowledge in which man finds it impossible to know and realize the revelation of God is the heart. "Neither have entered into the heart of man. . . ." The heart here represents the mind, the understanding, pure thought, the reason. We learn by observation through the eye; by tradition from others through the ear; and finally by our own reasoning. You can look around all you want, you can hear everything that history has passed on to you, and you can reason day and night, but you will find it impossible through these means alone to experience the power that resides in the gospel of the cross of Christ.

Disappointed and puzzled, you may use your rational powers to ask, "What and where is God?" You ask almost in vain of others who are your intellectual equals. A heathen philosopher, on having a similar question put to him, desired two days in which to prepare an answer. Partly pressed with the difficulties of the subject itself, and partly encumbered and confounded by polytheistic prejudices, he doubled and redoubled the time. When required to state the reason for his delay, he acknowledged, "It is a question in which my insufficient reason is lost. The more often I ask myself, 'What is God?' the less able I am to answer." How much more are you unable to reason out why an omnipotent God, in order to save your soul, had to become man in the person of Jesus Christ and die on a cross. That is beyond reason but within grasp and experience.

A Christian once served on a parliamentary commission with Professor Thomas H. Huxley. One Sunday they stayed together in a little country inn. "I suppose you are going to church this morning," said Huxley. "I am. I always go to church on the Lord's Day," replied the Christian. Huxley said, "Suppose you sit down and talk with me about religion—simple, experimental religion." Sensing something of heart hunger in the great scientist, the associate replied, "If you mean it, I will."

Then he spoke out of a rich, experimental knowledge of the saving and satisfying power of Christ. Huxley listened intently. Grasping the hand of the Christian, he said with deep feeling, "If I could believe what you have said about the cross of Christ and His pardoning love, I would be willing to give my right hand." He really did not have to make that sacrifice. All he had to give up was the belief that the eye, the ear, the mind, could know all that there is to know and experience. Had he only been willing to swallow the pride of reason and to accept God's revelation, he too could have experienced the power of God unto salvation.

Welcome into a Prepared World

The remark, "I accept the universe," has been attributed to a woman named Margaret Fuller. When Carlyle heard of it, he declared, "By God, she had better!" The remark may sound profane to our ears, but whether Carlyle meant it so or not, it contains a profound theological truth. Everything that exists was made "by God," and man must accept the world in which he lives as it is, or find himself fighting a losing battle. I do not mean he is not to try to improve conditions that are inimical to man, but he cannot change the fixed order of nature.

In his first letter to the Corinthians, Paul told them that they could not possibly discover by their physical senses, or through their traditional heritage, or their power of reasoning what God had prepared for man in the sacrifice of Christ on the cross. "Eye hath not seen, nor ear heard, neither have entered into the heart of man, the things which God hath prepared for them that love him" (1 Cor. 2:9). That phrase, "which God hath prepared," referring to the things that man cannot discover by his unaided powers, implies that they really do exist. They are there, and they are available. But God has predetermined how they must be appropriated. As there is only one way in which oxygen can be inhaled, so there is only one way in which the revelation of heaven, things prepared by God, can be appropriated by man. That is by faith activated by the Spirit of God.

Remember, Paul is thinking primarily here of the riches and glory that God has prepared for us in the person of Jesus Christ, the only riches and glory that really endure, and he wants us to understand that these riches can reach us—not through eye and ear—but through the Spirit of God who searches out for us the deep things of God. The natural man can neither see nor hear these things. The spiritual man, the man upon whom the Spirit has been outpoured, understands and knows them, for he has the mind of Christ. Just as the mind of an animal cannot understand the mind of man, the mind of the natural man cannot understand the nature and actions of God. God, says Paul, has prepared great things for those who love Him—and they can only do that through faith in Christ.

That God is a God who prepares things for us is true even in the physical world. Remember, there is a significant parallel between the physical and the spiritual worlds. Before we appear on the scene of this life, God has prepared for our coming. Just imagine if there were no oxygen in the atmosphere before our coming into the world, or if God had not given us the proper organ by which to breathe. The preparation had to be exact and minute.

In those things that God has prepared for us in the physical world, He does not give us much choice. They are fixed by Him, and there is really nothing we can do about them. We have nothing to say about our birthplace, our parentage, our color or nationality, our physical and mental endowment, and our spiritual heritage. Nor is there any such thing as equality among men in these fixed things. These are problems each of us must face. How we figure these things out for ourselves shapes for us our peace of mind, our usefulness, and our happiness in life. Quite easily these fixed things can fill us with discontent, misery, and discouragement. In the final analysis, it all depends on what view we take of God.

If we believe that God prepared them for us, meant them for us, we can adjust ourselves to them in a proper spirit and find peace. If, on the other hand, we believe ourselves victims of circumstance, then I do not see how this life can be anything other to us than a confused tangle, a series of events without rhyme or reason to them. Ask yourself seriously what you really believe.

From the biblical standpoint there is nothing else that we can believe, but that God prepared this world into which we have come. God as Creator prepared the world for men. The length of time in which He took to do it is not the important point, whether literal 24-hour days or eons. What really matters is whether you believe that things just happened or that God created the world. What matters is whether you believe that God is in the world, over it, above it, and through it—whether, in a word, you accept it as the work of His hands, and see in it the arrangements He has made for you.

Every discovery that modern science makes is just another proof that an intelligent, omnipotent mind prepared these things for us. Nothing can be understood or trusted otherwise. Research would be impossible if laws that govern the physical world were not prepared by Someone who knows far more than we can ever know. You step into a prepared world and you must ask the big question, "Where did all this come from?" for as Plato said, "The unexamined life is not worth living."

All that science can tell us is, in essence, what the Scriptures declare, that the eye cannot see God, nor the ear hear Him, nor can reason give any shape to Him nor describe Him. The five senses are not enough to enable us to know Him. If we are to know Him at all, it can only be through a sixth sense through faith. "For we walk by faith, not by sight" (2 Cor. 5:7). God gives us sight that through faith we may turn it into sight. "Through faith we understand that the worlds were framed by the word of God, so that things which are seen were not made of things which do appear" (Heb. 11:3).

But why has God prepared these things for us? For our edification and enjoyment. Why does a mother prepare a meal for her children? For their nourishment and enjoyment. Through what she prepares she develops her relationship with them. The world that God has prepared for us is for our feasting. Nature is God's table prepared for us. "Thou preparest a table before me" (Ps. 23:5). Nature to the child of God is a feast, a sacrament of wonder, of beauty, of order, of intelligence. God has spread His table for us in the sky above, in sunrise, sunsets, clouds, and storm. God has spread His table over the sea. God has spread His table over the fields. How foolish we are if we do not often sit down at nature's table of the Lord, or wander with the painter, poet, scientist, and naturalist among the quiet places where beauty dwells. The poet, Alice Mortenson, felt something of this, when she wrote:

> Oh, the loving kindness of God, whose sovereign will
> Could pause to make, for you and me, a yellow daffodil!

Are You Ready to Keep Your Final Appointment?

You and I have come into the world without having had any choice in the matter. We are here because of the will of our parents, and above all because of the will of God. We find a world that is prepared for us. What we prepare for ourselves is a very infinitesimal part of the whole of nature which God has spread before us like a table. In Psalm 23, David testified that the Lord had prepared a table for him in the presence of his enemies. In addition to those human enemies who sought to take his life, he may well have been thinking of the challenge of God-prepared nature.

We, too, must cope with nature: with storm and rain, heat and cold, hunger and thirst, plague and pestilence, death and disease, poverty and plenty. These are just some of the enemies of man. And they, too, are prepared for us that they may call forth our courage, our endurance, our intelligence, and our determination to persevere to the end. Unfortunately they sometimes call forth our complaints, our anger, our bitterness, and our despair. It all depends on how we face the challenge God offers us.

God's first word to us through these things He has prepared for us is *strive;* then *endure,* and finally *enjoy.* Not till we have striven and endured do we learn fully to enjoy. It often seems very hard to us. But surely God means to be hard on man only that He may call forth the best in him. God does not want us to go about pitying ourselves and seeking pity from others. Whether we like it or not, tribulation is part of God's challenge to us. Christ said, "In the world ye shall have tribulation: but be of good cheer; I have overcome the world" (John 16:33). By His grace we can overcome all difficulties and be victorious. "Thanks be unto God, which always causeth us to triumph in Christ" (2 Cor. 2:14). Let us believe that life is a great gift from God's hands, and into God's hands let us commit it. He who has prepared it for us can assuredly see us through it.

But would God have prepared a world for us without also preparing a way of salvation by which our estrangement from Him could be bridged and healed? We could not prepare such a bridge ourselves, for, just as we could not build the world, so we could not provide for our own salvation. If we do not accept the salvation God has provided, we cannot go through this world without being beaten by it.

From the beginning to the end of the Bible, runs the thought of God preparing salvation for man. We see what steps He took

from before all time to meet man's deepest and most fundamental need—redemption. We see how God chose a man, a
family, a nation, and a people to prepare the way for the Son of
His love. We trace a progressive revelation culminating in Jesus
Christ, who was foreordained from before the foundation of the
world to be our Savior. For His Son, God prepared forerunners
in the prophets and the wise in Israel, ending with John the Baptist, His immediate forerunner. He prepared Mary to be His
mother, Nazareth to be His home, Palestine His country, the
Jews His race; and He prepared the time for His appearance.
Nothing was so carefully prepared as the coming of the Son of
man, who came, suffered, bled, and died to bring us to God.
How can time ever be long enough to tell of the riches of His
grace stored up in Him who is the wisdom and the full salvation
of our God?

Even as we are to feast on the natural provisions God has
prepared for us, so we are to feast on the spiritual provisions made
for us by Christ. What He has prepared is a sacrament as well as
a challenge. Christ is God's sacrament of love for us. We are to
feast on Him. "Verily, verily, I say unto you, Except ye eat the
flesh of the Son of man, and drink his blood, ye have no life in
you" (John 6:53). Think of that. Christ is food unto eternal life.
This food is all prepared for us. If you are spiritually starved, it
could be your own fault. You could be like a child who refuses to
eat the good meal his mother has prepared for him. What a challenge Christ offers each of us to either accept or reject Him!

Think of yet another thing God has prepared for you. You
may not want to think of it, but it is unavoidable. "It is appointed
unto men once to die, but after this the judgment" (Heb. 9:27).
God has made the appointment, and you and I must keep it. We
sometimes think it strange that death should lie at the end of
man's earthly course, but it would be an infinitely stranger
world if it did not. Imagine a world in which no one dies—all

aging and none dying. It would be a world beyond measure wearisome, decrepit, and decaying. How different your attitude would be if you were to regard death as the portal to a bliss that is impossible to imagine—if you have already taken the salvation also prepared by Christ. What a place that must be—prepared for those who love the Lord! But without Christ in us, how can anyone be anything other than afraid to die?

I was speaking to someone in the presence of my editorial assistant, telling him, "Mrs. Bryant recently lost her husband." She immediately corrected me by saying, "No, I have just lent him to the Lord." What a beautiful way to face death—as a God-prepared appointment. At the funeral service of Lloyd Bryant, who loved and served his Lord, the following poem was read, which speaks volumes. It is entitled, "From a Loved One in Heaven," and I can only give part of it.

> I would not have you grieve for me today,
>   Nor weep beside my vacant chair;
> Could you but know my daily portion here
>   You would not, could not, wish me there.
> I know now why He said, "Ear hath not heard."
>   I have no words, no alphabet,
> Or even if I had I dare not tell,
>   Because you could not bear it yet.
> So, only this—I am the same, though changed,
>   Like Him! A joy more rich and strong
> Than I had dreamed that any heart could hold,
>   And all my life is one glad song.
>   —Martha Snell Nicholson

The wonderful things of nature and of the Spirit which God has prepared are only for those who love Him, however. Paul makes this plain when he calls them "the things which God hath prepared for them that love him." In the Greek text the wording is *tois agapōsin,* "those loving him," a present participle indicating continuous love. The more you love God the more He means to you and the more He will give you of what He has prepared for you in time and eternity (see James 1926, 110:220–22.)

LESSONS:

1. We cannot fully realize the glory of the unseen except as it is reflected from the things of earth, and it is only as we use earthly things that we become capable of seeing the eternal things that they signify.

2. The atonement accomplished by the Lord Jesus Christ on the cross is the fundamental difference between the gospel and all other religious systems.

3. Paul teaches that there is a spiritual faculty available to men which can make them wiser in the things of the spirit than all that the wisdom of this world knows.

4. The convicting power of the Holy Spirit enables a man to appropriate the power of God unto salvation.

5. God has prepared the world for us for our edification and enjoyment.

6. Let us believe that life is a great gift from God's hands, and into God's hands let us commit it. He who has prepared it for us can assuredly see us through it.

1 Cor. 2:10

God's Privileged Revelation

"But God hath revealed them unto us by his Spirit."

Do You Belong to God's Privileged Class?

Do not be surprised when I tell you that God has a special class of people to whom He reveals more than to others. I am only repeating what the apostle Paul says in 1 Corinthians 2:10, "But God hath revealed them unto us by his Spirit." Actually in the Greek text this verse begins with *hēmin de,* "unto us nevertheless," or "but unto us." "Those things which eye hath not seen, nor ear heard, neither have entered into the heart of man. . . . but unto us God hath revealed them." By the personal pronoun "us" Paul meant himself and all believers—those who had entered the kingdom of God, who were saved by receiving the crucified Christ. Speaking to His disciples, the Lord once said, "Unto you it is given to know the mystery of the kingdom of God: but unto them that are without, all these things are done in parables" (Mark 4:11).

The special revelations to which Paul referred were the hidden truths, the mysteries of God's nature, His providence, and His actions. To the natural man who is estranged from God through inherited and personal sin, God does not reveal these things about Himself. It is like looking at the stained glass windows of a church. To one who stands outside they seem dull and opaque, without meaning. But to one who looks at them from inside all is transformed. The lines and figures appear in all their rich loveliness. It is the same with the truths of God's Word. They are not attractive to those who are without. People sometimes sneer at the faith of Christians, as they find them leaning upon an unseen God and clinging to seemingly intangible hopes. But when one becomes a Christian all is changed. Where there was no loveliness there now appears the greatest beauty. What was laughed at before is now seen to be worthy of highest admiration. Only those who have accepted Christ can really understand the wonderful things of His love (Miller 1897, 190).

To those down here on earth, God's people often seem to be a downtrodden group. But their special privilege lies in the fact that God reveals to them His secrets and the end that awaits them. Notice the words of our Lord to His disciples on three occasions when they were being persecuted. The first instance is in Luke 12:2, "There is nothing covered, that shall not be revealed; neither hid, that shall not be known." The second is in Matthew 10:26, "Fear them not therefore: for there is nothing covered, that shall not be revealed; and hid, that shall not be known." And the third is in Mark 4:22, "There is nothing hid, which shall not be manifested; neither was anything kept secret, but that it should come abroad."

On each of these occasions our Lord was speaking of His kingdom and of the contrast between its modest, humble, hidden beginning and its glorious destiny. According to Matthew and Luke, the Lord said this to His disciples in order to comfort and encourage them. They were not to be afraid of the disproportion between their forces and the forces being arrayed against them, nor of the public position into which their allegiance to Him would inevitably lead them. The disciples needed to know that God was with them revealing to them that they were destined to triumph utterly and publicly in the end. It is as if our Lord were saying to them, "Life is indeed a mystery, but someday nothing will remain a secret from you."

One of the greatest privileges in becoming a believer is gaining God's confidence. Just imagine God letting you into His secret purposes! You remember what God said of Abraham, the patriarch of faith: "Shall I hide from Abraham that thing which I do?" (Gen. 18:17). God was going to destroy two wicked cities. He took Abraham into His confidence. Not only did God tell Abraham, but He also listened to Abraham's solicitude and intercession for Sodom and Gomorrah. What the Lord wanted to impress upon His people and the prophets of old was that, in proportion to their intimacy with Him, the mind of God would be unfolded before them, and His purpose would be made plain to all. "The secret of the Lord is with them that fear Him" (Ps. 25:14).

Think back to that occasion on which the rest of the disciples pleaded with John, who reclined upon the bosom of the Master, to ask the Lord to reveal something they wanted to know. They would not venture to ask the Lord themselves. The fact is, John became a kind of intermediary for his brethren. He lived so much nearer to Christ than they, that they asked him to bear their message to the Master and ask the Master that the secret might be revealed. Because John lived nearer to Christ, he shared more of His secrets (see Farmer 1927, 73–83).

Life can become so much more meaningful if we recognize God's secret intent even in the smallest details of our lives. To see God's revelation, to recognize God's provision in a loaf of bread on your table, for instance, and pause to thank Him for it, brings so much more joy to life than to recognize His hand only in such great deliverances as being snatched from certain death. Do you recognize God's hand in every gift and thank Him for it? How we need to adopt the attitude expressed by Robert Murray McCheyne in these lines:

> When this passing world is done,
> When has sunk yon glorious sun,
> When we stand with Christ in glory,
> Looking o'er life's finished story;
>> Then, Lord, I shall fully know,
>> Not till then, how much I owe.
> Chosen not for good in me,
> Wakened up from wrath to flee;
> Hidden in the Savior's side,
> By the Spirit sanctified;
>> Teach me, Lord, on earth to show,
>> By my love, how much I owe.

Did you ever wonder why the Lord revealed so much more of the future to John, His beloved disciple, than to anyone else? The Revelation John received from Him was not given to him to share with everyone in the world. It would not mean anything to them. Read the first verse: "The Revelation of Jesus Christ, which God gave unto him *to shew unto his servants* things which must shortly come to pass." The word "servant" here, *doulos,* means "bond-slave." Only those like John who have entirely sold themselves to Christ are admitted to His secrets. The closer your fellowship with Christ, the greater His revelation to you (see Chown 1877, 12:273–76).

The Only One Who Can Probe God

Just as you and I have certain people we love so much that we confide in them, so does God. And as there are certain things in our individual lives that some people will never discover, so there are certain things about the nature and providence of God that some people cannot and will not discover. But God does select certain ones to whom He will reveal His secrets. That is what Paul tells us in 1 Corinthians 2:10, "But unto us [that is, the believers] God has revealed them through the Spirit."

The word "revealed" in Greek is *apekalupsen,* which is made up of the preposition *apo,* "from," and *kaluptō,* "to cover." The verb signifies to take the cover off something, to unveil it, to lay it bare so as to expose it to view. Paul is speaking in this chapter of Christ's death for our salvation. It is the meaning of this fact of history that Paul says God has revealed to those who are saved, those who love God. Man's unaided vision could never have seen anything beyond that cross except the execution of a criminal. To tell us all that is involved in that fact, God had to speak, and He did speak.

A great many people find it extremely difficult to accept Christ's death on the cross as sufficient ransom for their sins. They want to do something themselves. "But I cannot see it," said a certain cabinet maker to a friend who was trying to show him how the death of Christ completed the work of atonement. At last an inspiration struck his friend, who, lifting a plane, made as if to plane the top of a beautifully polished table that stood near. "Stop!" cried the cabinet maker. "Don't you see that is finished? You will simply ruin it if you use that plane on it." "Why," replied his friend, "that is just what I have been trying to show you about Christ's work of redemption. It was finished when He gave His life for you; and if you try to add to that finished work you can only spoil it. Just accept it as it stands—His life for yours—and you go free."

No matter how clever a man may consider himself, he cannot grasp unaided the simple meaning of that simple fact. He needs an energy outside of himself to enable him to understand and accept it. If we could have discovered the meaning of the cross, it would not have been necessary for God to reveal it to us. God does not waste His time telling us things we can find out for ourselves.

Though the cross of Christ was a fact observable by human eyes and traceable in history, its meaning and its effect upon human life cannot be seen by the human eye. Paul says that it is revealed "by the Spirit." It is not "by his Spirit," as the Authorized Version has it. There is no personal pronoun in the Greek text. It is *the* Spirit, the third person of the Triune God, that is referred to here. His special, but not exclusive, function is to make God's revelation known to man, and particularly to the spirit of man, as the following verse tells us. There must always be a correspondence between the teacher and the pupil. You cannot transmit something that is in your mind to an insect, such as an ant. An ant can communicate with another ant, but a man, in spite of his superior intelligence, cannot do it. God made man's spirit capable of receiving communications from the Spirit of God, who has a definite personal existence outside of man.

In order to show us that the Spirit is capable of communicating the meaning of the cross of Christ to us, and also the secrets of God to our spirit, Paul adds, "For the Spirit searches all things, even the depths of God." Now the word translated "all things" in Greek is simply *panta,* which means "all" in the neuter gender. It should not be restricted to "things" but should be taken as including people, experiences, physical phenomena, and spiritual realities. Everything under the sun and above it is searched by the Spirit of God.

The word for "search" is *ereuna,* which, when originally used of animals, meant "to sniff out" with the nose. It then came to mean "to investigate a matter.' Here it means the probing insight of God into everybody and everything. And Paul adds that this ability to penetrate also extends to the depths of God. Actually, the Greek text does not say "the deep things," as the translation has it, but simply "the depths." Does Paul mean to imply by this that God has a surface and a depth? I believe he does. God's depths are His thoughts, while the surface may be considered as His visible acts, easily seen and understood by the common people.

Paul tells us that the Spirit of God has an insight into everything, even the depths of God. By this he suggests that, as a man's own spirit alone knows the depths of his own nature, so the Spirit of God alone can know the depths of God, that is, the mysteries of the divine nature and the ways in which God works. "Depths" implies something that is unexpressed and has to be probed or brought to the surface. A man also has depths within him. Psychologists tell us that there is an immense region open to self-consciousness in ordinary people that is absolutely closed to another observer. To ordinary acquaintances you show but the surface of your being; or perhaps now and again you give them a brief glimpse into some secret chamber of your thought or feeling. But take your most intimate friend, and though you confide more to that person than anyone else has ever known of you, much that passes through your mind is never known to him.

If I alone can know myself, much more God alone can know Himself. If my spirit or self-consciousness alone can give account of what is in me, His Spirit alone can give account of what is in Him. Just as I speak of my self-consciousness, not wishing to imply that I and my self-consciousness are different, so we may conceive of the Holy Spirit as the Self-consciousness of God. God might say "My Holy Spirit," not so much to distinguish the Spirit from Himself, as being anything less than God, as to express His own being in the relation between Himself and the consciousness of Himself.

And if I realize that I cannot know my fellowman as his own spirit knows him, much more must I be profoundly convinced that I cannot intrude into the being of God; I can never venture to search Him or to know Him in the way that His Spirit knows Him. The self-consciousness of the Being who made the universe, even as we know it, is as far beyond our thought as our human self-consciousness must be beyond the thought of the indistinguishable amoeba which floats in the ooze of the sea.

LESSONS:

1. Although on earth, God's people seem to be a downtrodden group, their special privilege lies in the fact that God reveals to them His secrets and in the end that awaits them.

2. One of the greatest privileges in becoming a believer is gaining God's confidence.

3. The closer your fellowship with Christ, the greater His revelation to you.

4. If we could have discovered the meaning of the cross, it would not have been necessary for God to reveal it to us.

5. Paul tells us that the Spirit of God has an insight into everything, even the depths of God.

6. The self-consciousness of God who made the universe, even as we know it, is far beyond our human thoughts.

1 Cor. 2:11 | *How You Can Know God*

For what man knoweth the things of a man, save the spirit of man which is in him? even so the things of God knoweth no man, but the Spirit of God.

Man Cannot Judge the Intentions of Another Man

God has infinite and unfathomable depths: His thoughts, His intentions, the purposes of His actions such as the death of His Son on the cross. In 1 Corinthians 2:10 we saw that only God's Spirit can search the depths of God, and that in the case of man it is the same way. This is borne out by verse 11: "For what man knoweth the things of a man, save the spirit of man which is in him? even so the things of God knoweth no man, but the Spirit of God."

It is interesting to note the two different verbs used for "know" in this verse. "For what man knoweth [*oiden*] the things of a man. . . ." The Greek verb in this context refers to intuitive knowledge. This is not knowledge passed on from one person to another. I can learn a great deal about you when you tell me about yourself. I can learn things about God when someone tells me about Him or when He tells me about Himself in His Word. But that is not the kind of knowledge referred to here. No man knows by intuition alone all that is in another man. You

147

cannot tell by looking at him what his thoughts and intentions are. Only his inner consciousness, his spirit, knows all that is in him, because it is part of his personality.

The Spirit Teaches Man the Depths of God

In the second part of the verse, "Even so the things of God knoweth no man, but the Spirit of God," the word used for "knoweth" is *egnōken.* This verb in Greek refers to acquired knowledge, such as you and I gain throughout our lives. Again the word "things" does not occur in the Greek text but is understood. It refers to whatever pertains to God—His nature, His character, His works, and so on. No man can ever learn all there is to know about God. No man can ever teach you all about Him. Even the Scriptures can never teach you all that is in God, or all about His eternal plan. It is simply impossible, says Paul.

When we say, "Even so the things of God knoweth no man [*oudeis*]," we are not really accurate in our translation of the word *oudeis* in the Greek text. It means "no one," and refers to any created being. (See Zodhiates 1970, *Was Christ God?* 14, 15, 171, where he deals with this same word in John 1:18, "No one has seen God.") Since man is not as infinite and eternal as God, it is impossible for him to acquire a full knowledge of an Infinite and Eternal God. This word also has the meaning of "understanding." To understand is to know, and to know is to understand. No man understands God simply by observing Him in the course of history. Only His own Spirit understands God. For man, there may not appear to be any purpose in God's mysteries, but for His Spirit there is full understanding of the purpose of each action of God, including the crucifixion of His Son.

Now observe how Paul carries on the argument about the possibility of man knowing God. Though man cannot *acquire* such knowledge and understanding, there is a way by which God can be known. Since the Spirit of God knows the depths of God, in order for man to know God intuitively he must have the Spirit of God within him.

LESSONS:

1. Two different Greek verbs used respectively for "know" in 1 Corinthians 2:11 are *oiden,* meaning intuitive knowledge and *egnōken* meaning acquired knowledge.

2. Since the Spirit of God knows the depths of God, in order for man to know God intuitively, he must have the Spirit of God within him.

1 Cor. 2:12 | *Heaven at God's Expense*

Now we have received, not the spirit of the world, but the spirit which is of God; that we might know the things that are freely given to us of God.

How You Can Receive Life's Greatest Treasure for Nothing

In the 12th verse Paul goes on to say, "Now we have received, not the spirit of the world, but the spirit which is of God." What is the spirit of the world? The word "world" here is not the same as the word *aiōn* of verses 6, 7, and 8, which are translated "world" in the Authorized Version. Instead it is *kosmou*, which refers to the material world, whereas *aiōn* means "age, epoch, period." The spirit of the world is the spirit or understanding of material things. Materialism can never enter into the depths of God, for God is Spirit. He is beyond material comprehension because He is not material.

Of course, by the word "we" Paul refers to himself and all who are believers. Their natural minds do not help them at all to comprehend God. Verse 12 continues, "But the spirit which is of God; that we might know the things that are freely given to us of God." Again the verb translated "know" here is *eidōmen*, intuitive knowledge. In other words, when we receive the Spirit derived from God, that is outside of ourselves, the immediate result is that we intuitively recognize and understand the gifts that God gives us in Christ—the greatest of these, of course, being our salvation through His death on the cross.

Thus Paul teaches that the Spirit, the self-consciousness of God, can be and is imparted to the Christian, so that in some limited degree this Spirit produces or reveals in us a knowledge of His being. No matter who you are, it is possible for you by simple faith in Christ to receive the Holy Spirit and to know God. That Spirit that moves from without us to within us cleanses and transforms the human self-consciousness, and in that transformation illuminates. The Spirit thus communicated, by effecting a renewal of human nature, renders a knowledge of the divine nature possible.

Take Paul as an example. We recognize that his insight into the Being of God was due to the Holy Spirit within him. And we as Christians know what occurs when by faith in Christ we receive the Holy Spirit. We cannot be saved without the Holy Spirit entering into us, because only the Spirit of God within us gives meaning to the cross of Christ. It is through this Spirit within us that we are introduced into the Being and the Life of God. We are conscious of His currents pulsing through us. God is no longer a mere supposition, required by our minds to explain the universe. He is no longer a mere Lawgiver brought in from without to explain and justify the authority of conscience or the moral law. God is now intimately experienced. Whatever certainty attaches to our own being now attaches to His. We become certain that He is in us and that we are in Him. The self-consciousness of God has come into us and is now intermingled with our self-consciousness. We are inducted into His nature and are led to live His life.

The things of time, the vanishing shows of earth, now assume their right proportion. As moments in the development of the divine plan, they have their interest and their reality, but we recognize that they are transient. They cannot occupy much thought or desire beside those things which eye sees not and ear hears not, and which enters not into the heart of man, the things God prepares for them that love Him. For these are the things which God reveals to us by His Spirit.

A once-popular song bore the refrain, "The best things in life are free." All of us recognize that there are things money cannot buy, including life itself. It did not cost you anything to come into this world. And your ability to see, to speak, to think, to hear, to walk, to grasp, and many other fundamental aspects of life came to you as gifts. You did not work for them nor could you have worked for them.

Why then are so many people skeptical when we tell them that the greatest spiritual possessions of life can be free too? Why insist that they must be acquired through personal effort and merit? Salvation, forgiveness of sins, the peace of God, the knowledge that He loves you, a sense of belonging to Him—these are spiritual values. They are treasures freely bestowed by God on those who come to Him through faith in Christ. You cannot acquire them through your own efforts.

One of the main objections of the natural mind to the gospel of Christ is that it seems too cheap. How can something that you can get for nothing be worth anything? Yet these same people breathe free air every day without thinking that it cost them nothing. If they found themselves where it was un-available, they would realize how precious air really is.

A miner once said to a preacher, "I would like to be a Christian, but I cannot receive what you said tonight." "Why not?" asked the preacher. "Well, I would give anything to believe that God would forgive my sins, but I cannot believe He will for-give me if I just turn to Him. It is too cheap." The preacher looked at him and said, "Have you been working today?" Sur-prised, the man replied, "Yes, I was down in the pit as usual.

Why?" "How did you get out of the pit?" "The way I usually do. I got into the cage and was pulled to the top." "How much did you pay to come out of the pit?" The miner looked at the preacher in astonishment. "Pay? Of course I did not pay anything." "Well," said the preacher, "were not you afraid to trust yourself in that cage? Was it not too cheap?" "Oh, no," he said; "it was cheap for me, but it cost the company a lot of money to sink that shaft." Then the implication of what he had said struck him, and he saw that though he could have salvation without money and without price, it had cost the infinite God a great price to sink the shaft to rescue lost men.

Look carefully at the expression, "the things that are freely given to us of God," in 1 Corinthians 2:12. The phrase "the things that are freely given" in Greek is one participle, *ta . . . charisthenta*, "the ones donated to us." The word "things" does not appear in the Greek text. This participle does not refer to mere things as we speak of them but to those most valuable experiences that cannot be seen by the eye, or heard by the ear, or felt by the heart. It is above all the experience of salvation through the crucified Christ. It has no reference to material things but to things that belong to the realm of man's spirit which is the moving part of his entire personality. Happiness is not something material. It is a spiritual value that pertains to attitudes, to the disposition of the spirit of man. You may have every material asset and yet be miserable. The participle *charisthenta* is related to the noun *charis*, meaning "grace," and the verb *charizomai*, meaning "to give freely or graciously as a favor, to donate." Charisma is a word much used nowadays to indicate the gift or gifts of the Holy Spirit. It is something that is freely given, not having been earned by the recipient. Spiritual gifts, are not human acquisitions but are donated by the Holy Spirit. They are actually the result of the indwelling of the Holy Spirit within the human spirit.

Paul teaches that a Christian is one in whom the Holy Spirit dwells. The Greek text of verse 12 says, "And we received not the spirit of the world, but the spirit which proceeds from God." The word "proceeds" is not in the text but is understood. The actual Greek text is *to ek tou theou*, "the one out of God." There is a spirit that belongs to the world (*to pneuma tou kosmou*), which is the spirit that characterizes the world and its thinking. This is the spirit that thinks that nothing so precious as forgiveness of sin and salvation can cost the recipient nothing. That is the natural thinking of man. That is why all other religions, including the perverted Christian religions, seek in effect to buy their salvation through sacrifice, penance, and good works. Heathen religions placed their confidence in sacrifice. Perverted Christianity places its confidence in good works and human merit. But true Christianity teaches that salvation is free because of the sacrifice of the Lord Jesus Christ on the cross.

"Neither by the blood of goats and calves, but by his own blood he entered in once into the holy place, having obtained eternal redemption for us. . . . how much more shall the blood of Christ, who through the eternal Spirit offered himself without spot to God, purge your conscience from dead works to serve the living God?" (Heb. 9:12, 14). Notice the mention of the Spirit here.

In speaking of that Spirit of God that comes into man, the expression is rather different in the Greek text. It is "the spirit the one from out of God." He is a personality who comes out of God to be given to man. The verb "received," *elabomen*, which is in the second aorist, and which refers to the spirit of the world, also applies to the receiving of the Spirit that comes out of God. It indicates that this receiving was a definite acquisition at some time in the past. You received the spirit of the world when you were born into this sinful world. Your thinking concerning God was perverted from the very start. You could not know the depths of God, the nature of God, His plan for your salvation.

But when you are born again by the Spirit of God, His Spirit comes into you and your thinking is changed. All that you have, you now consider as a gift from God. Once you thought yourself master of your own life. Now you realize it is all of grace. The Spirit of God within you enables you to see more and more of the depths of God. Once you may have thanked God for material things only. Now you thank Him for Himself and His spiritual gifts as well: salvation, forgiveness of sin, and a new nature. A great man was asked what was the most important lesson he had learned in life. His reply: "To take things with gratitude and not take them for granted." The thing that will make you more grateful than anything else the moment you receive the Spirit of God within you is that salvation is free and that it is a great treasure.

How to Lose Your Fear of This World's Darkness

The apostle Paul said in 1 Corinthians 2:10 that the Spirit of God searches the depths of God. Then in verse 12 he says that those who have believed in Christ have received the Spirit that is from God so that they can know those things that have been freely given to them by God. What are these things freely given by God? They are the depths of God which His Spirit searches. Therefore we who are believers are able also through the indwelling Spirit of God to know the depths of God. This is a tremendous privilege for any man.

To begin with, there is the depth of the divine nature that is revealed conclusively and finally by the incarnation of the Eternal Son. That God is three distinct persons, God the Father, God the Son, and God the Holy Spirit, is a depth of God rejected by the wisdom of the world but fully accepted by the believer through the indwelling Spirit of God. Man's natural mind cannot accept the truth that God is One, and yet three persons. It is the Spirit of God within a man after he has believed that reveals this to him as the depth of God, and leads him to accept it as beyond human reason yet a reality, as so many other realities even in the physical world are beyond him.

It is evident that the distinctions of Father, Son, and Spirit are established in the usage of the New Testament. The discourses of the fourth gospel present the Son speaking to the Father and promising to send the Spirit. "And I will pray the Father, and he shall give you another Comforter, that he may abide with you forever; even the Spirit of truth; whom the world cannot receive, because it seeth him not, neither knoweth him [*ginōskei*, knowing by learning and investigating]: but ye know him; for he dwelleth with you, and shall be in you" (John 14:16, 17). You see, therefore, the futility of arguing with an unbeliever about the depth of the nature of God as being three persons in one. He can never see it until he is born again of the Spirit of God.

The apostolic writings also reflect almost unconsciously the threefold name. In 1 Corinthians 12:4–6, for example, the three names might be the names of a single agent: "There are diversities of gifts, but the same *Spirit*. And there are differences of administrations, but the same *Lord* [that is, Christ]. And there are diversities of operations, but it is the same *God*." Or again in Ephesians 4:4–6, the language insensibly expresses the revealed fact: 'There is one body, and one *Spirit*, even as ye are called in one hope of your calling; one *Lord*, one faith, one baptism, one *God* and Father of all." And the familiar benediction taken from 2 Corinthians 13:14, "The grace of the *Lord Jesus Christ*, and the love of *God*, and the communion of the *Holy Ghost*, be with you all," secures the recognition of the same fact in our congregational worship.

It is no less evident that these distinctions did not, in the mind of speaker or writer, conflict with the unity of God. No one was ever more confident than Jesus that there is one God, and that God is one. And Paul is most particular, even in the passages quoted, to lay stress on this oneness by adding to the name of God the clauses, "which worketh all in all" (1 Cor. 12:6, where the "who" is singular, not plural); and "who is above all, and through all, and in you all" (Eph. 4:6). Although the word Trinity does not occur in the New Testament, it may be said to *be* the New Testament. The Old Testament may be described as the manifold, historical, poetical, and prophetic assertion of the One God. The New Testament is the revelation of the Trinity in the One God.

There is a second depth of God which the believer accepts the moment the Spirit of God indwells him: the depth of the incarnation and the deep beyond the deep that is revealed by God the Son suffering on the cross for us and for our redemption. The depth of God, unveiled in the life and death of Christ, is of such a kind that men for the most part are hardly sufficiently equipped to understand it. Many who saw the cross of Christ, many who still contemplate it, are equally unreceptive. They do not have enough spiritual insight to see anything more than the death of a man, a good man, the best of men, a miscarriage of justice, a human tragedy.

But as the Spirit begins to search and to illuminate, there appears here a wonder that may even engage the curiosity of angels (1 Pet. 1:12), a wonder that has entranced the devout minds of these twenty centuries, and has by its enlarging influence made these minds the greatest power of their time. For, guided by the Spirit, we discover that the incarnation implies the eternal being of God as love, a relation between Father and Son that existed before the world began and will continue after the world has ended. The cross implies that the love which is God is the love that goes out beyond, creating and redeeming; a love that makes men in His image, a love that will save them even by suffering and death. To this depth of love you can only bow as the Spirit energizes you.

Paul tells us that there are other depths of God that come within the grasp of the believer. In Romans 11:33 he says, "O the depth of the riches both of the wisdom and knowledge of God!" When you realize the wealth of God that is yours through the Spirit, then material wealth takes an inferior place. The appropriation of the depth of the wisdom of God places all human philosophies under your feet. Through it you escape the baffling inconclusiveness of scientific conclusions that tell us everything about the universe except what it exists for and whence it sprung; everything about human affairs, except the goal that makes them intelligible; and everything about men, except the things that distinctively make him man.

Through the Spirit within you, you can escape the terror of the infinite universe. This world is a wilderness to a godless spirit, but to the believer it can be turned into a home by an intimacy with God who fills it. You then feel like that little boy of four who laughed as he pulled aside the curtains to find the source of a suspicious noise. "Who's afraid of the dark?" he said. "There is nothing but God in the dark!" That is the height of human discovery, and it is made when the Spirit of God searches within us the depths of God and makes us familiar with them. Then "Perfect love casteth out fear" (1 John 4:18; see Horton 1901, 1–5, 21–35).

LESSONS:

1. The natural man who objects the gospel of Christ because it seems too cheap, costing him nothing, is the same one who breathes the air everyday without thinking of its freedom.

2. Happiness is a spiritual value that pertains to attitudes, to the disposition of the spirit of man.

3. Perverted Christianity places its confidence in good works and human merit, but true Christianity teaches that salvation is free because of the sacrifice of the Lord Jesus Christ on the cross.

4. The thing that will make you more grateful than anything else the moment you receive the Spirit of God within you is that salvation is free and that it is a great treasure.

5. The Old Testament may be described as the manifold, historical, poetical, and prophetic assertion of the One God, whereas the New Testament is the revelation of the Trinity in the One God.

6. When you realize the wealth of God that is yours through the Spirit, then material wealth takes an inferior place.

1 Cor. 2:13	*How You Can Be Spiritual, Yet Human*

Which things also we speak, not in the words which man's wisdom teacheth, but which the Holy Ghost teacheth; comparing spiritual things with spiritual.

Be Careful What Words You Use to Proclaim the Gospel

The apostle Paul ascribed all that he knew about the mysteries of God to the Holy Spirit within him. In 1 Corinthians 2:7 he says, "But we speak God's wisdom in mystery." The Greek word for "speak" here, as we saw in previous studies, is *laloumen*, indicating that we give voice to something without necessarily trying to explain it. That is good reasoning, of course, in speaking with unbelievers, since God's wisdom would be a mystery to them.

Then in verse 10 Paul says that the things inconceivable by the natural mind have been revealed to him and to others who have received Christ. That is because the Spirit of God who searches the depths of God comes to indwell the believer. Therefore he too is now able to search the depths of God and know them in the measure that the Holy Spirit permits. Romans 8:16 says, "The Spirit itself beareth witness with our spirit, that we are the children of God." God's Spirit and our spirit are definite and separate identities, but there is also agreement between them. Before a man believes, there is disagreement between God's Spirit and his. But this changes after he believes. Then the spirit of man becomes subject and obedient to the Spirit of God.

In the Old Testament the phrase used to indicate this agreement between man's spirit and God's Spirit is "the fear of the Lord." In Psalm 25:14 we read, "The secret of the Lord is with them that fear him; and he will show them his covenant." That is exactly what Paul is telling us in 1 Corinthians 2:6–15. These two passages indicate that there is a certain "organ," so to speak, of spiritual discernment in the soul of the believer, both under the old covenant and the new, of which the natural man is not possessed—a certain condition of mind or state of feeling without which the believer cannot hold communion with God and become the subject of spiritual illumination. There are certain experiences—hopes and fears, joys and sorrows—which depend entirely on the relation in which we stand to God. If the heart be cold and dead, still unrenewed by the Spirit of God, it is impossible for us to understand the meaning of fellowship with God and with His Son, Jesus Christ. But if the heart has been touched by divine grace, and that great eternal change of the new birth has taken place, without which it is impossible to see God, then it is not only possible, but a matter of common experience with believers that God does reveal Himself and fills the heart with joy unspeakable and full of glory.

In the Old Testament, the man who had undergone this change obtained the character of one who feared God. "Then they that feared the Lord spoke often one to another: and the Lord hearkened, and heard it, and a book of remembrance was written before him for them that feared the Lord, and thought upon his name" (Mal. 3:16). In the New Testament he obtains the character of a new man, one who is born again and has become a new creature in Christ Jesus. He has received the organ of spiritual discernment, so that, just as the eye is the organ of sight and performs the function of seeing, this spiritual organ performs the function of apprehending spiritual truths.

These truths, Paul says in verse 13, we also speak. The first part of this verse in the Authorized Version reads, "which things also we speak." But the word "things" as such is not in the Greek text. Instead, we have the relative pronoun *ha* in the neuter gender, "which." This may refer to experiences, truths, depths of God, whatever fails to fall into the apprehension of the natural mind. Now these truths become part and parcel of us and we proclaim them. The word for "speak" here is the same Greek verb *laloumen* found in verse 7, meaning to speak without attempting to explain these truths to which Paul refers, for, no matter what explanation we may give, the natural mind of man will not appreciate it. It is all foolishness to him in spite of the fact that it is the wisdom of God.

Paul explains, first negatively and then positively, the way this message of truth is to be proclaimed. "Not in words which man's wisdom teaches." That is the negative side. "But [in the words] which the Holy Spirit teaches, comparing spiritual things with spiritual." That is the positive side. Remember that *laloumen* here means to speak without necessarily trying to explain the message of truth. You do this when you yourself may be unable to explain something, or when you realize that the person to whom you speak does not have the ability to comprehend it. Just as it would be foolish to try to explain the solar system to a small child, it is equally as foolish to explain redemption through the death of Christ to an unbeliever. The reason Paul just "spoke out" the gospel without trying to explain it was that the natural mind cannot comprehend the things of the Spirit of God. Therefore he says in effect, "I and other apostles proclaim the gospel [just tell it forth as it is], not in words that are taught by human wisdom."

The word translated "taught" is *didaktois* in Greek, an adjective derived from the verb *didaskō,* "to teach." It refers however to "that which may be taught." Paul wants us to realize that the gospel given by the Spirit of God cannot be dressed in human wisdom. It loses its power to save. This verse reinforces my opposition to God's Word, the Bible, being translated by men who may be excellent scholars but are not born-again Christians filled with the Spirit of God. That is why I do not recommend any Bible translation that has been made by men who have brought to their work only their own natural wisdom.

This verse also leads me to believe that Paul and other writers of the Bible did not go out of their way to borrow terms and words from heathen philosophers to convey God's revelation to man. Paul says we are to use "words taught by the Spirit." This indicates that the Holy Spirit not only gives the content of the message to be proclaimed but also teaches what words to use to proclaim it.

Primarily, Paul is speaking here of himself and the other apostles who, having seen Christ after His resurrection (1 Cor. 9:1), gave us the New Testament writings. This is his definite statement in favor of the verbal inspiration of the Scriptures. Paul believed that not only the message of the Bible, but also the very words used in the original tongues, were inspired by God's Spirit. The message cannot be correct and the words wrong. They are both correct, and they are both inspired. You do not need men of worldly wisdom to teach you the Bible. The greatest teacher is the Holy Spirit.

How You Can Be on Intimate Terms with God

A young woman who was soundly converted immediately began to read her Bible. One who disbelieved the Scriptures and took delight in ridiculing them asked her, "Why do you spend so much time reading a book like that?" "Because it is the Word of God," replied the girl. "Nonsense! Who told you that?" scornfully asked the unbeliever. After a moment's silence the girl asked, "Who told you there is a sun in the sky?" "Nobody," replied the scoffer; "I do not need anybody to tell me. The sun tells me." "Yes," said the girl in triumph, "and that is the way God tells me about His Word. I feel His warmth, and sense His presence as I read His wonderful Word!"

That is exactly what Paul was getting at when he spoke of "comparing spiritual things with spiritual." But that is an unfortunate translation of what he really wrote. The Greek word *pneumatikois* with which this last phrase of 1 Corinthians 2:13 begins refers to *logois*, "words" (dative plural and agreeing with *didaktois*, "taught"). Words that are taught by the Spirit of God are spiritual words. The word translated "comparing" is *sunkrinontes* in Greek, which occurs only here and in 2 Corinthians 10:12. The meaning is rather "evaluating, interpreting, expounding" (Kittel 1965, 3:953–54). Thus we would have "expounding spiritual things or experiences or truths in or with spiritual words." Paul declares that there must be an agreement between what is conveyed and the means that convey it. The message of the gospel must not be expounded in merely philosophical terms, in words of human wisdom. We may compare this to conducting water through pipes of the proper material to insure that the water will not be polluted.

We are not to look for human, natural wisdom in the Bible. The words have spiritual meaning and pertain to spiritual realities and experiences. That is why, to the unregenerate mind, they do not mean much. The man who has not been born again cannot begin to understand them, though they are so simple.

Not possessing the Spirit of God, he is at a loss to understand spiritual realities expressed in spiritual terms. Paul says that changing our terminology will not do any good. What is needed is a change in the hearts and spirits of those who read and hear the Word of God. Again this is what Psalm 25:14 teaches: "The secret of the Lord is with them that fear him; and he will shew them his covenant." Therefore, in order that you may understand the Word of God, you must start fearing God. But how do you go about it, and just what is this fear?

When the psalmist speaks of the fear of God in you that will enable you to enter into the secrets of the Lord, he is not referring to morbid fear, but to reverence and awe. It is the attitude that a properly disposed child has toward an earthly parent. Though he loves his father and has entire confidence in him, he fears to displease him; for the thought of his parent's displeasure is a greater pain than actual punishment. That is how to draw near to God—as children draw near to a father; and we are told that "Like as a father pitieth his children, so the Lord pitieth them that fear him" (Ps. 103:13).

It is in this sense that the "fear of the Lord" in Psalm 25:14 is to be understood. It is the equivalent of what Paul says in 1 Corinthians 2:9 when he refers to "them that love him," or tells us that the Spirit of God dwelling within the human heart understands the depths of God. It represents that disposition of mind that inclines us to render Him all the worship He requires, to submit to all the Laws He imposes, and to conceive all the emotions of admiration, devotion, and love that the character of His perfections demands.

What a wonderful privilege those indwelt by God's Spirit have! As they read His Word they hear Him speak and can understand what He says. They have communion and fellowship with God. A man who has the friendship and confidence of great and famous people enjoys a distinction of which he is proud. Just imagine then what a greater distinction and privilege it is to be in the confidence of God, to be admitted to His secrets. If you do not enjoy that experience in your own heart, do not blame God. Remember, the transmission of His secrets is couched in spiritual terminology. Are you spiritually attuned to Him? Do you belong to that select group of people whom God delights to honor with His confidence, and to whom He reveals Himself from day to day with a personal and delightful intimacy? The greatest blessing that can come to man is to be on terms of intimacy with God.

For those of us who look on the Lord Jesus Christ as the perfect revelation of the Father, that "selective freedom of God," as George Morrison called it, is abundantly confirmed and illustrated. There is no soul that Jesus is not willing to save; there is no man whom Jesus does not love; there is no sheep crying in the wilderness whom the Shepherd will not leave His flock to rescue. Yet, universal as His mercy is, Christ, like that Father whom He came to reveal, had His special, more intimate friendships. Out of the multitude who trusted Him, He chose twelve to be His special comrades. Out of the twelve He made a choice of three to be with Him when He was transfigured. And then out of the three He singled out one, John, who has been known down through the centuries as "the disciple whom Jesus loved." Though Christ would have been welcome in many homes, out of all the homes in Palestine He chose a home in Bethany, the home of Lazarus and his two sisters. He loved them in a special way. They loved Him, too, but they also revered Him. Why these choices by the Lord? The secret of the Lord was with them that feared Him. He had His intimate friends and special confidants. There were certain men and women to whom He revealed the treasures of His heart.

There is a different quality, however, to such intimacy. It is mixed with adoration and awe. We have a proverb that says, "Familiarity breeds contempt." You never become so familiar with God as to order Him to do things for you, or utter words such as, "Come on, God, let us go." God is still God when you become His intimate child. Always distrust that light familiarity with the Almighty Maker of the universe that regards Him as a "Buddy." When speaking to Him, always assume a respectful posture. He who is closest to the throne is on his knees. You have the wisdom of God if you act with fear, with reverential awe, in His presence, yet with the intimacy and confidence of a child (see Morrison 1912, 366–76).

Do You Really Enjoy God? If Not, Why Not?

Christians fall into two distinct classes. On the one hand we have those who have been born of the Spirit of God and have thus become His children, but who remain atrophied in their spiritual development. They do not grow sufficiently so that God can communicate with them on an adult basis. He "spoon-feeds" them, as it were, but they do not enjoy close fellowship with Him.

The second class consists of those who thrive on God's Word, advancing from "baby-food" to the real "meat" of His Word on an adult level, and finding keen joy in their fellowship with the Lord. It is in such fellowship that God reveals His secrets, His depths.

Both of these classes of Christians are going to go to heaven, but it is not reasonable to believe that both of them will enjoy it equally. The enjoyment of heaven, I believe, will depend to a great extent on the intimacy of our fellowship with God here on earth. The deeper we enter into His secrets, the more we shall enjoy Him—both here and hereafter. God reveals Himself to those who fear Him, to those who in reverential awe seek Him out and make Him the center of their thoughts and actions. You cannot enter into the secrets of God by pursuing human wisdom. You can only do it by waiting upon God.

Then again, God may want to reveal His secrets to you, but before He can do so there must be an intercommunity of interest and feeling, a mutual understanding and sympathy, that intimate

knowledge that one person has of another so that the one is said
to be in on the secrets of the other.

Suppose, for example, a group of men are engaged in discussing the conduct and policy of some public figure. The ends
he has in view, the probabilities of failure and success, are debated
and analyzed. One man takes a pessimistic view, declaring the
person's motives are bad, the plan impracticable, and the whole
scheme sure to fail. Another stoutly defends both the motives
and the chances of success. Then a third party comes into the
room, listens to the arguments pro and con, and settles the
whole matter by declaring, "I know this man personally, and I
can vouch for the fact that his motives are good, his policies
sound, and that he is solidly informed on all the issues involved in this particular undertaking." At once the atmosphere
changes. The others realize that here is a person who has an intimate knowledge of the man himself and so can speak with authority of his thoughts and feelings. This is the ground of the
authority with which Paul and the other apostles spoke forth the
Word of God concerning the character and the depths of God.
"We speak in words of God's wisdom" (1 Cor. 2:13). The
greater your knowledge of the depths of God, the greater the authority with which you can speak.

You do not know another person's secrets unless you maintain friendship with him. True friendship is based on a similarity
of views in regard to all important questions, whether social or
religious, such as respect for each other's convictions, a marked
liking for each other's society, a strong defense of each other's
reputation and interests when these are assailed, warm affection,
perfect trust, and thorough sympathy with each other. In other
words, there has to be similarity between two characters before
there can be intimacy between them. Such intimacy over the
years enables them to understand each other as no other human
being ever can. The joy of one is the joy of the other; the sorrow

of one is the sorrow of the other; the interest of one is the interest of the other. In short, they know each other's secret self; they possess each other's love and confidence; and that is what is known by the name of friendship.

This helps us to understand what Paul is trying to convey to the Corinthians concerning the Holy Spirit's teaching and entrusting us with God's secret. The man who fears God possesses God's secret. He enjoys the favor and fellowship of God. Between his spirit and God's there is a closeness of sympathy that must be felt to be understood. It is inward, practical, experimental.

As we look at such a man externally, we do not see much to distinguish him from other professing Christians. He is ethical in business, keeps his word, fulfills his obligations, and his private life is exemplary. But there are many professing Christians who are as upright in business, as much to be trusted, and as correct in their private habits, so where does the difference lie? They both belong to the Christian Church, and are both apparently interested in the cause of Christ.

Yes, externally, one professing Christian may be very like another, but internally, where the eye of God alone can see, the difference can be very great. One man is upright from a sense of honor, the other man from a sense of love for God. The one sees things merely as right and wrong, while the other sees them as pleasing and displeasing to God. It makes a tremendous difference whether your life is motivated by strict orthodoxy or by a love that knows the very secret recesses of the heart of God. Externally the worshipers are alike, but the great Searcher of hearts is there, revealing Himself only to those who fear Him. Just as a radio station can only communicate with those who turn their dial to its wave length, so God speaks to those who are open to receive His secrets. Spiritual words are received by spiritual people, and they result in spiritual experiences that fill the heart of the believer with joy unspeakable and full of glory.

When the church service is over, a spiritual person may be heard to say in all sincerity, "I felt the presence of the Lord; my soul was refreshed; and my spirit rejoiced in God my Savior." Those who give expression to language such as this possess the secret of the Lord. They may not be able to explain it, and no wonder, for it is often too deep for utterance. It is a peace that passes all understanding; it is a love that passes knowledge. Still, such experience is no mere fiction. The people of God everywhere will bear witness of its truth; and if they are skeptical regarding it, the only explanation is that their hearts are not yet rightly disposed toward God and therefore cannot become the subjects of His illumination.

The same truth applies to our private devotions as to our public worship. While the nominal Christian may be said to pray, he does it as a sacred duty. He touches only the circumference of God, not His depths. But the Spirit-filled Christian prays not merely from a sense of duty but because he feels prayer to be a most precious privilege, a necessity of his spiritual life, the atmosphere of his heart, its vital and vivifying breath.

LESSONS:

1. The Old Testament person who feared God is the same as the New Testament person who is born again as a new creature in Christ.

2. Paul just "spoke out" the gospel without trying to explain it because the natural mind cannot comprehend the things of the Spirit of God.

3. The message of the gospel must not be expounded in merely philosophical terms, in words of human wisdom.

4. He who is closest to the throne is on his knees. You have the wisdom of God if you act with fear, with reverential awe, in His presence, yet with the intimacy and confidence of a child.

5. The enjoyment of heaven, I believe, will depend to a great extent on the intimacy of our fellowship with God here on earth.

6. The greater your knowledge of the depths of God, the greater the authority with which you can speak.

1 Cor. 2:14 | *Why Not Everyone Can Understand Spiritual Truths*

The natural man receiveth not the things of the Spirit of God: for they are foolishness unto him: neither can he know them, because they are spiritually discerned

The Limitations of What Your Soul Can Know

One day Mark Twain took his little daughter on his knee and told her all about the rulers and other prominent men whom he had met in his travels. She listened attentively. When he had finished she said, "Daddy, you know everybody but God, don't you?"

Mark Twain was certainly an intelligent person. Yet he rejected God. You are probably acquainted with many such people. They seem to be reasonable and intelligent human beings, and yet, when it comes to God and His revelation, they simply reject them. Things that are clear and valuable to a believer are incomprehensible and unacceptable to them. Do not get provoked with them. Their rejection of things divine is only a natural reaction to what they are. The apostle Paul clearly states this in 1 Corinthians 2:14: "The natural man receiveth not the things of the Spirit of God: for they are foolishness unto him: neither can he know them, because they are spiritually discerned."

Who is this "natural man" of whom Paul is speaking? In the Greek text, the word translated "natural" is *psuchikos*. This is an adjective derived from the noun *psuchē,* which means "soul." The English word "psychology" comes from this word also. Psychology is the study of the soul and its reactions to life. In the Scriptures, soul sometimes refers to the immaterial part of man, often including both elements of his immaterial self—that is to say, the soul or the animate nature which he holds in common with animals, and the spirit which is a kind of higher compartment of his spiritual self, a window upward which enables him to know God.

As far as man is concerned, the word *psuchē* or "soul" and the word *pneuma* or "spirit" may be used interchangeably to refer to the immaterial part of man, and when one is referred to it may very well include the other. For instance, whenever man's soul is said to be comforted by God, this includes not only his soul but also his spirit, that particular element in man with which God is able to communicate. The same thing is true when his soul is said to be cast down, as in Psalm 42:6, "O my God, my soul is cast down within me." This, of course, includes the spirit of man. To see this more clearly, examine John 12:27, where the Lord says, "Now is my soul [*psuchē*] troubled." And a little later on, when the Lord foretells His betrayal, we read in John 13:21, "When Jesus had thus said, he was troubled in spirit [*pneuma*]." On the other hand, no earthly creature other than man is said to possess a spirit in the sense that man has. The spirit of the beast tends to go downward (Eccl. 3:21). That is why animals do not know God nor can they praise Him or complain against Him. Only the spirit within man is able to communicate with the Spirit of God. Job 32:8 tells us, "There is a spirit in man"; and Zechariah 12:1 refers to "the Lord, which stretcheth forth the heavens, and layeth the foundation of the earth, and formeth the spirit of man within him."

The term *psuchikos* referring to man in the Scriptures means the man who is governed only by his environment, by his natural or animal instincts, by his fallen Adamic nature. The word *psuchikos,* "the natural or soulish man," occurs in 1 Corinthians 2:14, twice in 1 Corinthians 15:46; in James 3:15, and Jude 19. In the Authorized Version it is translated as "natural" or "sensual."

Psuchikos is to be distinguished from another Greek word that is also translated "natural" in English. The word is *phusikos,* derived from *phusis,* which means "nature, the physical world." We get the English "physics" and "physical" from this word. *Phusikos* occurs only in Romans 1:26, 27 and 2 Peter 2:12 (where it is translated "natural"). Observe how two distinctly different Greek words have been rendered: *psuchikos* (soulish) and *phusikos* (physical). *Phusikos,* "physical or natural," should never be translated "soulish." *Phusikos* applies to something that is caused by the material element of man, whereas *psuchikos* applies to something produced by the lower of the two nonmaterial elements of man, the soul which he holds in common with the animals.

Psuchikos, the soulish man, therefore, is the man whom Paul describes as being "in Adam." It is the man who is estranged from God because of Adam's sin. When a person becomes a new creature in Christ Jesus, he is then said to be "in Christ," and he becomes a spiritual being, *pneumatikos.* This means that, although he had a spirit within him before he believed, that spirit was dormant. He was spiritually dead. It is as if he had an atrophied organ that could not serve him. He had a pilot light, but it was not lighted. The supremacy of his immaterial being was held by his soul, his animal self, so to speak, and not by his spirit, his higher self, which is on God's "wave-length."

Paul taught in 1 Corinthians 15:45 that the man Adam compared with the man Jesus was a defective and preliminary type of manhood. The one was "a living soul," the other "a quickening spirit." What is the difference? It may be compared to the difference between the ground which receives the seed and the sun which pours out its vitality and quickens it into life. Though ground and sun are necessary to the germination and development of the life of the seed, the ground is not the sun, nor the sun the ground, yet each is necessary to the other. In the light of the apostle Paul's teaching, Adam in his fallen state did not represent God's fully developed man. As Adam he is mortal. He is the earthly man, the man fitted for this earth only. But God's purpose was to make a man who would be fitted for continuous life, beyond the here and now, not merely for the earth life.

There are two classes of people in this respect, the natural and the spiritual. The natural are what the Greek text of 1 Corinthians 2:14 calls *psuchikoi*, the soulish, those directed by animal instinct. The *pneumatikoi*, the spiritual, are those whose dormant spirit, rendered dead by the fall of Adam, is enlivened by the Spirit of God. The psychic man, then, is the one who is conscious only of what is going on around him, and not above him. The soul as distinguished from the spirit cannot know the things of God's Spirit; only the spirit of man can know anything of the Spirit of God.

Annie Johnson Flint wrote of those

> Who are dumb in the language of heaven
>   And have never been born again—
> To them the things of the Spirit
>   Are quite beyond their ken.
> Oh, the peace and the joy they are missing!
>   Eternal and infinite loss,
> If they seek not the life everlasting
>   And find not the way of the cross.

Why Men Reject the Gospel

The apostle Paul tells us that there are men who are all soul and no spirit, all creatures of environment living on the horizontal plane, with no vertical look or relatedness to God. To the man in whom the soul is all, the spirit is like a dark untenanted chamber. When Solomon built the temple it was constituted thus: outer court, holy place, Holy of Holies. The outer court corresponds to our body, the holy place to our soul, the Holy of Holies or most holy place to our spirit. In the regenerate man the most holy place is tenanted by the Spirit of God, but in the unregenerate man it is untenanted and dark, waiting for its occupant. The natural man is the one whose spirit is empty of God.

In contrast to the psychic or natural man is the spiritual man. This man is one who has a window looking upward, the man whose spirit is quickened by the Spirit of God, who wills and lives beneath the impulse of the Holy Spirit Himself. The spiritual man, then, is the one whose own spirit is dominated by the Spirit of God.

Just as a blind man would not be capable of studying the stars he cannot see, so is the spiritually blind person unable to search out or fathom the things of the Spirit of God. "He cannot know them," Paul declares emphatically. A natural man merely reveals his stupidity and ignorance when he tries to pronounce judgment on spiritual matters and experiences.

A medical doctor sitting in the company of friends quickly cut in on a lay person who, with an air of authority, was talking about a particular disease. "Only a specialist who has devoted his life to medical science is entitled to speak with authority," he declared. He was right. Before long, however, the conversation turned upon a religious question. Without a moment's hesitation the doctor became equally dogmatic. When it was politely pointed out to him that he had not made a study of the Bible and was not religiously inclined, he confidently voiced the assumption that all people are equally entitled to an opinion on questions of religious truth and experience. According to him, the person who hardly gave five minutes' serious attention to the claims of the Spirit was entitled to rank equally with those to whom the reverential fear of God was a daily study and passion.

Surely it is not difficult to see the fallacy of this; yet thousands of naturally intelligent people fail to see it. Such people attempt an exposition—yes, even at times an exposé—of a world outside their experience, which it is therefore impossible for them to understand. They are, so to speak, the blind who have instituted the astronomy of the blind. Their knowledge of astronomy would be based on mere hearsay, not on personal observation. Mentally such people inform themselves upon religious questions to a greater or lesser extent. They vaguely feel that there is another world around them, as in a vague way the physically blind are conscious of the sky, the sun, and the seasons. But they are not competent to pronounce on questions of the spiritual life, even as blind men are not competent to set themselves up as authorities on the phenomena of the heavens.

Our Lord repeatedly pressed this solemn truth upon the natural, soul-oriented theologians of His day—that through pride and worldliness they had become insensible to what was pure and heavenly. Of the Pharisees He said, "Let them alone: they be blind leaders of the blind" (Matt. 15:14); "Woe unto you, ye blind guides" (Matt. 23:16); "Ye fools and blind" (Matt. 23:17). In this manner He continually characterized those who aspired to become the religious teachers of their generation. These pseudo-guides could no longer see the face of God's heaven; and so they conceived an astronomy of their own in which the stars were placed and called by wrong names, a pretentious system calculated only to mislead and shipwreck whoever trusted in it. Nothing more aroused our Lord's anger than this astronomy of the blind with its fatal consequences.

Paul asserts that there is a divine wisdom that is not attained through the senses or by merely intellectual processes but is revealed by the Spirit of God. And this spiritual, supernatural truth is revealed only to spiritual men. The natural man cannot know such truth because he lacks the proper organ of recognition. Not, of course, that anyone completely lacks the faculty of spiritual perception that belongs essentially to our human nature, but in the natural man it slumbers; only the animal life is awake. That is why the new birth is sometimes spoken of in Scripture as a spiritual resurrection. It is only natural, therefore, that the great beliefs, ideals, pleasures, and hopes of the Christian faith often appear absurd to the natural man (see Meyer 1901, 75–76; Parker 1959, 210–17; Smeaton 1958, 62; Watkinson 1912, 17–29).

The reason the natural man does not receive the things of the Spirit of God is that he considers them foolish. Of course he exercises his will in refusing to accept them. His mind tells him not to, in spite of the fact that his heart may yearn for some relief from the burden of sin. The Greek verb for "does not receive or accept," *ou dechetai,* is somewhat different in meaning from *ou lambanei,* the verb used in John 1:12 that speaks of receiving Christ. The former indicates the rejection of something that is offered directly to a person, whereas the latter indicates something that is picked up as it lies down.

In other words, what the apostle wants to convey here is that the natural man is acted upon by the Spirit of God, who has a separate and distinct existence outside of man. That Spirit gives man the ability to choose God's offer of salvation through Christ's death. It is a definite offer to a definite person. And if that person chooses to reject the offer, he is responsible for the rejection. Why did he reject the offer? Because he wanted first to understand how it works. When he could not understand it, he dismissed it as foolishness. Your acceptance or rejection of the gospel determines its meaning for you.

> What will you do with Jesus?
> Neutral you cannot be;
> Some day your heart will be asking,

"What will He do with me?"
                    —A. B. Simpson

Are Christians Opposed to the Use of Reason?

The apostle Paul flatly declares that the natural man does not receive the gospel because he considers it foolishness. But he adds something else in 1 Corinthians 2:14. Furthermore, he declares, he cannot know the things of the Spirit of God, because they are spiritually judged or inquired into. The verb for "know" here is *gnōnai,* which refers to investigative acquired knowledge. The things of God's Spirit cannot possibly be experimentally tested for the mere sake of testing. You cannot set out to prove the rightness or wrongness of God's actions in human life. You cannot grasp with your human mind what God can do in you. You can only "know" (*eidenai*) God intuitively by allowing His Spirit to indwell and enlighten you. Spiritual things can be investigated only by spiritual means.

The word translated "discerned" in the Authorized Version is *anakrinetai* in Greek, which is a term indicating "legal investigation." *Anakrisis* even in modern Greek refers to the occasion on which a person appears before a judge to be examined. Since the things of God are spiritual and not material, they can only be investigated by a spiritual medium, which is the Spirit of God within man, who comes in when man accepts God's offer in Christ. The same Spirit makes the offer, and the same Spirit enables a person to accept the offer.

What Paul indicates here is that, even when you receive what the hand of God offers you through the cross of Christ, you must not think that the acceptance is entirely of your own volition and power. It is still all of the Spirit of God energizing your natural self to accept God's spiritual gift, His salvation.

Some people take this verse as grounds for accusing Christians of being opposed to the use of reason in matters of religion.

This is not true at all. A Christian thanks God for the reason He gave him, and he uses it properly in the realm for which it is intended. Each gift of God to man has a purpose, and it must be used as intended, or the results can be disastrous. Just as fire may be used to benefit or to destroy, so human reason, when used in its proper sphere, can direct us in making sane and sensible decisions in the natural world. But when it sets itself up as competent to judge spiritual matters, it is out of its depth and can only flounder and drown as a result of its own foolish presumption.

There is no hocus-pocus about the Christian faith. Has not God issued the invitation, "Come now, and let us reason together" (Is. 1:18)? The Christian faith courts investigation; it welcomes inquiry. It calls upon men to serve and love God not only with the heart and the soul but also with the mind. There was not a touch of the obscurantist about Paul. He himself brought a mighty brain to bear upon Christian truth. He was the thinker par excellence of the apostolic group. He would be the last in the world to challenge the function of reason or to deny the rights of the intellect. On the contrary, he commended the Christian's faith and service on the ground that it is essentially reasonable. First Corinthians 2:14, therefore, is not a denial of the rights of the intellect. It is not an assertion that the reason has no part to play in religion. It is simply an assertion that reason by itself is not enough, that something more than a keen and clever intellect is necessary for the discernment of religious truth. And there is nothing unreasonable in this apostolic contention. Paul is really only laying down a principle, the reasonableness and necessity of which are freely acknowledged in other spheres of human learning.

As a matter of fact, there is very little knowledge that has come to us as the result of pure reason. It is a great mistake to suppose that the acquisition of knowledge consists in the reception of certain bare facts by a blank mind. No mind is blank, and no facts are bare facts. We all assert that two and two are four. But can you really be sure that, if you put four men on a job, you are going to get twice as much work out of them as you did out of two?

There is hardly a science that can be strictly classified as a purely intellectual discipline. We come to the study of any and all facts with minds already full of presuppositions, predilections, and assumptions. If the process of knowing were simply the reception of bare facts into blank minds, all men would exhibit uniformity of thought and belief. But, as a matter of experience, we know that the same facts mean one thing to one man and quite another thing to another. And the reason for this is that our minds are not blank at all. Each of us looks at the facts through his own special and peculiar spectacles. The nature of a man's perception depends upon his personality. What a man knows depends upon what he is. His conviction depends upon his character. Knowledge, therefore, is not the result of mere intellect, but of emotional and moral factors as well.

We can readily understand that to appreciate painting you need much more than a clear eye and the power to distinguish colors. You need more than a brain. You need a certain moral and spiritual gift; you need a sympathy with the painter's mind and purpose. Likewise, to appreciate music you need more than an accurate ear; you need a little of the musical temperament, a bit of the musician's soul.

In the same manner, to understand men you need more than a clear head; you also need a sympathetic heart. It is no use, for instance, asking a man to write a biography of another if he is not in sympathy with his subject. A picture of a great man drawn by someone completely out of sympathy with him will not be a true picture, but a gross and lying caricature. To know a man thoroughly, intimately, you need to be in affectionate sympathy with him.

It is the same principle, the validity of which you acknowledge in everyday matters, that Paul is applying here to the matter of Christian truth. It comes to men, not through the mind only, but also through the heart, the emotions, and the will. To understand Christian truth you need more than intellectual cleverness; you need moral sympathy with the truth you seek to grasp; you need the Spirit of God. "These things are spiritually tested." The only difference is that, if the principle holds good in other spheres of human knowledge, it holds with tenfold validity in the apprehension of Christian truth. For Christianity is not just a theory, it is not just a set of maxims, it is not even a mere body of truth—although all of this is included. It is basically a personal relation, it is an obedience, it is a life. Christianity is in reality life in Christ.

Is Your Christianity a Creed or a Life?

Some people think that being a Christian means that you subscribe to certain beliefs, and that is it. But Christianity did not begin as a mere set of doctrines; it began as a vital experience in the hearts of men. Experience came first, dogma second. It was not the Christian dogma that gave rise to the Christian experience; it was the Christian experience that gave rise to the Christian dogma. Men felt certain things and then felt constrained to try to give an intellectual account of them.

Take the cardinal doctrine of the incarnation, for instance. The apostles did not start with the doctrine. They gathered certain impressions from their association with Jesus Christ and the works He accomplished in them. Seeking to account for those impressions and those mighty and revolutionary works, they understood and subsequently explained them by saying under the Spirit's special inspiration that Jesus was no mere man but was God manifest in the flesh.

Or take Paul's doctrine of the atonement. That is not a mere dialectical exercise, something evolved out of Paul's brain. Paul's theory of the atonement was drawn out of the blood and fire of his own experience. The crushing burden of sin, the ineffectiveness of law, the redeeming and life-giving power of the crucified and risen Christ—they were vital experiences with Paul before they were translated into doctrines. His doctrine of release through the atoning sacrifice of Christ is simply the attempt to give intellectual expression to what he had already experienced. Now, if that be the true order, it follows that for the true appreciation of these great Christian doctrines an identity of experience, a sympathy of spirit is required.

These things, Paul asserts, are spiritually tested. If Christian truth were purely intellectual, like the multiplication table, the intellect would be sufficient for its apprehension. But Christian doctrine is Christian experience translated into speech. To understand and appreciate the speech into which it is translated you must first of all have some sympathy with and some share in the experience. You must be a Christian if you are to understand Christianity. A share in Christian experience is the condition of appreciating Christian truth.

When it comes to the substance of the Christian faith, when it comes to the great spiritual verities that constitute Christianity, the competence of the mere critic to decide must be challenged. Mere scholarship is not enough to judge. If a man is to judge rightly upon these high matters, he must be more than a critic; he must be a Christian. He must be more than a scholar; he must be a saint.

How is a man to know who and what Christ is if he has never put himself in Christ's hands? How is a man to know whether the cross is the power and wisdom of God or not if he has never felt the ache and burden of his own sin? These things are spiritually tested, and a man who has no experimental knowledge of Christ, and who has never felt the sinfulness of sin, is as incompetent to pronounce judgment upon the incarnation and the atonement as a blind man would be to pronounce judgment on color or a deaf man on sound.

Over against the denials and negations of the critics we must set the experience of the saints. They know that Jesus is the Son of God, for they have felt His power in their lives. It should not trouble us very much that the mere critic sees nothing in these great doctrines of the gospel. The faith is secure because multitudes have found them true by experience. And the saint, the man who has made experiment, is the only competent judge of Christian truth. He is the true defender of the faith. The faith was delivered once for all, not to the mere critic or scholar, but to the saint, the one in whom Christ dwells.

The experience of the humblest laboring man whose life has been enriched and transformed by the love of Christ is of greater value than the abstract philosophy of the most eminent scholar in the world who, possessing no experience of such things, argues academically that they are nonexistent.

"I am by birth," said a converted Hindu, "of an insignificant and contemptible caste; so low, that if a Brahmin should chance to touch me, he must go and bathe in the Ganges to purify himself. Yet God has been pleased to call me, not merely to the knowledge of the gospel, but to the high office of teaching it to others." Then addressing a number of his countrymen he said:

> My friends, do you know the reason of God's conduct? It is this: If God had selected one of you learned Brahmins, and made you the preacher, when you were successful in making converts, people would say it was the amazing learning of the Brahmin, and his great weight of character, that were the cause. But now, when anyone is convinced by my instrumentality, no one thinks of ascribing any of the praise to me; and God gets all the glory.

Do you desire to know that Christ is the Son of God? Do you desire to know that the cross is the power of God to set you free from your sins and give you eternal life? Then come and put yourself in Christ's hand and let Him work His will in your life. Come and kneel at His cross, until both your sin and the divine love are revealed to you (see Jones 1926, 28–41).

> I have a life with Christ to live,
>   But ere I live it must I wait
> Till learning can clear answer give
>   Of this and that book's date?
> I have a life in Christ to live,
>   I have a death in Christ to die;
> And must I wait till Science give
>   All doubts a full reply?
> Nay, rather, while the sea of doubt
>   Is raging wildly me about,
> Questioning of life and death and sin,
>   Let me but creep within
> Thy fold, O Christ, and at Thy feet
>   Take but the lowest seat,
> And hear Thine awful voice repeat
>   In gentlest accents, heavenly sweet,
> "Come unto Me and rest;
>   Believe Me and be blest!"
>   —Principal Shairp

Are You Fit for Heaven?

What does the New Testament mean when it speaks of putting off "the old man" and putting on "the new man"? In Colossians 3:9, 10 the apostle Paul tells Christian believers, "Ye have put off the old man with his deeds; and have put on the new man, which is renewed in knowledge after the image of him that created him."

The "old man" is our sinful nature passed on to us by Adam. The "new man" is the new nature born within us when we receive Christ. Paul's writings are proof of these contrasts. He is constantly speaking of an "old" and a "new" and the relations of one to the other. In Paul's teaching, Adam stands as a type of the natural life. The Adam life is called the "old man" because it is a life that fails and fails again, with no recuperative powers in itself. The life of which Christ is the type is called the "new man," because it is ever young, ever new, and has in it the power of renewal and continuance. This is not a once-and-for-all renewal, but a constant one.

Paul teaches—and the rest of Scripture bears him out—that because a man is born into this world he is not a complete and perfect man, and this is why he is so unhappy. The complete and perfect man is the Christ man, the spiritual man, and not the soulish man. The imperfect and incomplete man is the Adam man, the one who lives only for this world and is directed by his soul and not by his spirit. Adam was fitted for this world's life but not for the heavenly life. This earth is completely unsatisfying if not lived with eternity's values in view.

There are many people who are fitted only for this world's life. Those who have no appreciation of, or sympathy with, the heavenly or spiritual life are not fitted for it either here or hereafter. It is wholly unreasonable to say that God is cruel not to give spiritual or heavenly life to those who do not receive it, have no desire for it, and are totally unfitted for it.

Actually what Paul declares in 1 Corinthians 2:14 when he says, "The soulish man does not receive the things of the Spirit of God," is that the soulish man is unfit for a spiritual environment either here or hereafter. The lower Adamic life, the soulish life, is unfit for the higher Christ life, the spiritual life. Before anyone accuses God of arbitrariness and cruelty because He is not going to receive everybody into heaven after they die, consider this illustration:

Suppose a man as a youth had the chance of getting a good education, but he preferred to waste his time with the gang in pool halls and on street corners. Now when he is a grown man and has the opportunity of entering into cultured and intellectual society, he has no pleasure in it and is totally unfit for it. He seeks his companions among those whose conversation never rises above coarse jest and uninspiring themes.

If he opens his lips in more cultured society, he only does it to reveal his inability to get along in such company. His unfitness excludes him; he voluntarily absents himself. No evening could be more miserable than one in which he had to spend hours in the company of cultured and intellectual people. They are quite willing that he should be there if he wishes, but their conversation makes him miserable. He lacks the ability to think their thoughts or speak their language, or even listen to it. He actually does not know what they are talking about. His exclusion is entirely a matter of unfitness.

Lewis Sperry Chafer states the following in his book, *He That Is Spiritual:*

> In this passage the natural man is not blamed for his inability. It is simply an accurate statement of the fact of his limitations. We have just been told that revelation is by the Spirit. It therefore follows that the "natural man" is helpless to understand things revealed, because he has not received "the Spirit which is of God." He has received only "the spirit of man which is in him." Though he may, with "man's wisdom," be able to read the words, he cannot receive their spiritual meaning. To him the revelation is "foolishness." He cannot "receive" it or "know" it.

The Greek verb translated "receiveth not," *ou dechetai,* is in the present tense, indicative mood, which would indicate that it refers to a man in his sinful state not receiving on his own volition and by his own power something specific that is offered to him. As mentioned previously in these studies, there is a distinction between the Greek word *lambanō,* "receive," which suggests a self-prompted taking—that is, one in which man takes the initiative—and the verb that we have here, *dechomai* (first person singular), which indicates a welcoming or an appropriating reception. It involves the offer of something specific first. In this context, it indicates the acceptance of something that is offered which involves more or less of a realization of its importance. It presupposes God's offer of salvation to man through the death of Jesus Christ. That there is knowledge involved in this acceptance or rejection is indicated by the second part of this verse, in which Paul says, "Neither can he know them." Know what? The spiritual realities, or the things of the Spirit of God, or spiritual truths that can cause him to be transferred from the sphere of Adam to the sphere of Christ.

The verb *ou dechetai*, "receiveth not," definitely presupposes an offer of something. It is a response—although in this case a negative one—to the initiative which God has taken in perfecting the imperfect soulish man by enlivening the dead spirit in him through the Spirit of God. You can never pride yourself on discovering God, because becoming a spiritual man, or being born again or saved, is nothing but responding to God's initiative in salvation. You will never know what the Spirit of God can do in you until you permit Him by faith to do it. If you wait until you can understand the deep things of God, as Paul calls them, you will go on forever in your natural state without tasting the incomparable joy of the Christ life.

Paul indicates that there is a relationship of the soulish or natural part of man to the spiritual part. The Bible teaches that the Creator meant the body for the sake of the soul, and the soul for the sake of the spirit. The proper life of man is spiritual in quality. And if you ask what is meant by spiritual life, the answer is, the life that recognizes its obligation to and dependence on God for everything, and that strives to live in harmony with that recognition. To possess this life, one must receive the Spirit of God without question, knowing full well that the soulish self is incapable of understanding or receiving by itself the things of the Spirit of God.

Why Some Men Cannot Believe in a Biblical Heaven

The ancients believed that somewhere there existed a fountain of perpetual youth. Like all beautiful dreams, it had its origin in the desire of the human heart to live on, free from the debilities and losses that age brings. The life of the spirit, when once it is generated and established, knows no age. Age touches only that which is composite, and can be separated into its parts. The life of the spirit is not like that of the body. In every man there is a process of bodily growth going on all the time, and by and by the material body can no longer serve the uses of the spirit and falls off. Immediately, the spirit discovers itself spiritually embodied and in the spiritual world—a world which:

> *Lies about us like a cloud, a world we do not see;*
> *Yet the sweet closing of an eye may bring us there to be.*

The fact of the renovating power of a godly life was never recognized by anyone more beautifully than by the psalmist who wrote, "Bless the Lord, O my soul, and forget not all his benefits: who forgiveth all thine iniquities; who healeth all thy diseases; who redeemeth thy life from destruction; who crowneth thee with lovingkindness and tender mercies; who satisfieth thy mouth with good things; so that thy youth is renewed like the eagle's" (Ps. 103:2–5).

In a truly godly life there is always a newness, a freshness, a recuperative power not found in the old Adam life. That old Adam life is the life the apostle Paul calls "natural," not because it is the life God intended for men, but because it is, as it were, a part of the nature that is around us to which it belongs. It is part of that which fades and vanishes away. The eternal life, of which we see the best illustration in the Lord Jesus Christ, does not fade and vanish but has within it that which is imperishable.

The Mount of Transfiguration gave the disciples a new idea of the nearness of the spiritual world. God had only to close their fleshly eyes and open their spiritual eyes, and there stood Moses and Elijah with Jesus, who seemed glorious because they no longer saw merely His body but His very self. Every spiritual man, every "new man," as Paul calls him, is living all the while in a spiritual world as far as his spirit is concerned, and the reason he does not recognize it is because of the veil between it and him, that is to say, his flesh, his soul.

When we regard the Adam life, then, as the ground in which the Christ life is sown, it has the same relation to it as the soil to the seed. In His very first parable our Lord calls the truths and facts about Himself "seed" which is sown on various kinds of ground. Man's nature provides that ground. The truth as it is in Christ is the seed. And when it finds good ground—receptive ground—it produces the new life of the new man. In the creation of the new man from the old man, the old is not useless; it is preliminary to the new. You cannot have the new without the old, as you cannot have the new rose without the old stem and root and the old ground in which it is planted. And though we cannot say that we find in the people walking our streets two different human natures in different men, there are men of two basically different characters, because there are two creations. There is the "new man" or the spiritual man, and the "old man" or the soulish man. The first man has become new, has become regenerated, because his spirit is alive, because he has then submitted himself to the regenerating influences of the Spirit of God.

However, the man who is still the Adam man, though very well fitted for the present conditions of life, is fitted for nothing better than what now appears. He is a man whose sole aspiration oftentimes is to be an amply enriched man of this world.

His idea of heaven, if he consents to accept such an idea at all, is a material garden of Eden providing physical, not spiritual, pleasures—a physical heaven with enough to eat and drink, no physical pain, no disease; a place where neither medical doctors nor doctors of any kind are needed. Beyond physical conditions his mind never rises, his ambition never aspires. Such a life cannot continue. By its very nature it is perishable. This man thinks such a condition is good enough for him. The spiritual germ sown in his nature remains unfructified. He has resisted those influences of the Spirit of God that would cause it to spring up to fruition. The new life is to him a dream, if not a fear.

When Jesus met Nicodemus, He spoke to him of this new life as essential to seeing and entering the kingdom of God. "Except a man be born from above, he cannot see the kingdom of God" (John 3:3). The idea was entirely new and perplexing to Nicodemus. His mind had been trained to think that to be a descendant of Abraham and to conform to Jewish tradition was enough, that all that was needed was to be born in the chosen nation and to accept the common theology of his time. When the Lord started talking about being born from above, he was baffled and startled, and his very language shows how materialistic his thinking had become. Virtually the Lord said, "The physical life is for the sake of the soul life, and the soul life is for the sake of the spirit life." Until a man lives the spiritual life, he is incomplete; and if he remains continuously in that state he will be a total failure, just as the apple blossom which never results in fruit is a failure. The Adam man is preliminary and preparative, the Christ man is the complete and perfect type.

There is a parallel between the physical and the spiritual. The fittest for one condition may not be the fittest for another condition. How can that which is soulish receive that which is spiritual? Our Lord suggests the possibility of a man gaining the whole world, becoming a Caesar or an Alexander, the world at his feet, the master of armies which hold it in slavery, and yet losing his own soul. The word soul here stands for his spirit or his spiritual element of life, which is the real life in man. Man may become the fittest of all and the most prosperous of all in his Adam life, but this is of absolutely no use in the spiritual world. If he develops his soulish life without developing the spiritual life offered him by God, he is not a gainer but a loser. He cannot enter the kingdom of heaven. He is unfit for it. On the other hand, when any man comes under the power of this new life, all parts of his nature become illumined and energized. And some men are so interpenetrated with this inward life that the difference between them and the Adam men is the difference between the red-hot iron all aglow with energy and glory, and the same iron, gray and dull and all the fire gone out of it.

A Microscope through Which You Can See God

A good illustration we could use for the spiritual life indwelling the soulish or physical life of man is that of extracting what we call electricity, that subtle fluid or energy, from matter. The whole residuum would be as a measureless heap of cold gray ashes. This electrical force seems to be representative in the material world of spiritual force in man's spirit. That which separates man from the intelligent creatures below him is just this spiritual force. Animals do have minds, and they do possess reason of a sort, although it is inferior to man's. But they do not possess a spirit that can be activated by God's Spirit. There is a difference, and a radical difference, between the spiritualized man and the animal. It is the spirituality that makes the difference. So far as a man conforms to the Adam type, he is still the animal man; so far as he conforms to the Christ type, he is a spiritual man, a complete man, the man whom God meant him to be when He said, "Let us make man in our image, after our likeness" (Gen. 1:26; Thomas 1893, 44:113–15.)

By the phrase "natural man" in 1 Corinthians 2:14 Paul did not necessarily mean a person more wicked than others, one who was entirely given over to moral corruption. A natural man is rather one who may be endowed to the fullest of his nature with understanding, sense, and capacity as a creature of intellectual and physical life. This term, "natural man," refers rather to a person who has never been born again by the Spirit of God. Therefore he lacks that higher spiritual understanding that the Spirit of God imparts. He cannot see or discern spiritual things because they are above his ordinary and natural life.

A scientist gives this illustration from the physical world. In describing the intricate beauty and mysterious structure of a leaf, he says that any amateur can see the facts for himself by procuring a leaf and a microscope. But how helpless he would be if he had only the leaf and not the microscope. The leaf would be perfect in all its minute parts; it would continue to possess rare beauty of form, color, and structure, though the amateur remained ignorant of it, not having the instrument with which to see it. Even the science teacher, lacking a microscope, could not see the mysterious substance, the strange maintenance, and the beautiful structure of the leaf. The optical instrument is as necessary for the intelligent as for the ignorant, for the scientific as well as for the uneducated. If a man were to examine the leaf without the aid of a microscope and declare his inability to see any inner beauty, form, and structure in the leaf, the simple reason would be that these are things which can only be microscopically discerned.

The apostle Paul was in the most profound sense truly scientific. He taught that without the proper spiritual instrument—the Spirit of God within you—it is impossible for you to discern spiritual realities that exist outside of you. Spiritual truths can only be discerned by a spiritual mind—a mind aided and strengthened by the higher power of vision that the Spirit of God imparts. That is why the natural man cannot receive the things of the Spirit of God, for he lacks that higher power of spiritual faith so necessary to enlarge his vision and to enable him to see what, by the ordinary powers of the natural man, he could not see.

Without a microscope we can see the leaf and understand somewhat of its uses and qualities, but not its full beauty and purpose. Likewise, without the Spirit within us as our spiritual organ of vision, we cannot discern or perceive the things of the Spirit of God. True, we may arrive at the conclusion that there is a God of some sort, but we can never know the intent and disposition of God toward us, and the purpose of God in time or eternity. We may recognize a truth such as the death and resurrection of Christ, but we cannot see the purpose of it and how it affects our own life.

We have a wonderful revelation of God in Jesus Christ, in His life and death as recorded in the Gospels. That revelation is not in itself obscure or difficult or mysterious. The things of Christ are not hidden from us, except if we are among the lost, those whom the god of this world has blinded.

If we do not see the light, it is not because there is any imperfection in the light. No, it is a defect of our vision or a closing of our eyes that prevents us from seeing. The revelation of God in Jesus Christ is the light of God that is outside or external to us, and the Spirit of God must illumine our souls within us if we are to see the light outside us and take it into our being. Though Christ is the channel of the Father's revelation to men, the highest revelation does not in one sense come to us directly from Christ. It comes to us by our contact with the Holy Spirit who touches our minds and spirits. This is the doctrine of the New Testament proclaimed by Christ and His apostles. Christ said that the Spirit "shall take of mine [that is, the purpose for which I came into the world, died, and rose again], and shew it

unto you" (John 16:15). We may add, however, that we cannot
have Christ without having the Holy Spirit, or the Holy Spirit
without having Christ.

Spiritual things were hidden from the wise and prudent and
revealed to babes. Unconverted Nicodemus scarcely understood
earthly things, so that Christ declared He could not speak to him
of spiritual things. According to Paul, those things that the
natural eye has not seen, nor the natural ear heard, nor the natural heart understood, God has revealed to us by His Spirit. As
man knows the things of man only by the spirit of man that is
within him, so the things of God can be known only by the
Spirit of God coming to dwell in man.

This is not only the teaching of Scripture, it is also the teaching of all human life. If we had no spirit of beauty within, no
taste in our eye, we could walk through the art galleries of the
world and see only pictures on canvas, without ever discerning
the intent of the artist or the feeling he meant to convey to us.
A musician could fill the air with melody that would make his
own soul flow with the richness of harmony. But though he
might fill our ears with sound, yet through our lack of musical
knowledge he would be unable to carry us along with him into
those regions of thought and emotion that flood his own soul
with delight.

And so, through all life, we discern only that for which we
are prepared by the state of our spirit. Truth is truth the world
over, whether we discern it or not; and this is so most profoundly
with spiritual truth. But the Spirit of truth, the Spirit of God
Himself, must be in us in order for us to discern the deep things
of God.

God Cannot Be Like That! Or Can He?

What is God like? One of the main stumbling blocks in finding an answer to this question is that we have a strong tendency

to let our own ideas impose themselves upon the facts, instead of letting the facts impose themselves upon us. Quite unconsciously we conceive of God in our own image. It is instinctive and proper for the human heart to seek God. But the danger is that we will only find the God we want to find. Such an impulse has to be balanced by the realization that God is seeking to speak to us; and that if that were not so, all our seeking would be in vain—and that it is not what we say but what He says that is important. Unregenerate religion always tends to say, "Hear, Lord, for thy servant speaketh." Regenerate religion tends to say, "Speak, Lord; for thy servant heareth" (1 Sam. 3:9).

"God cannot be like that," is a statement made in ignorance born of wishful thinking, if it is not based on the self-revelation of God in His Word, the Bible. The apostle Paul was given a more intimate personal revelation of God's nature, intents, and purposes than almost any other scriptural writer. He tells us, through the use of the expression, "the things of the Spirit of God," that God is a spiritual being. He is characterized by ineffable goodness and love. He has been from all eternity, and will continue throughout all eternity, to be the same loving, compassionate God whom Christ revealed in His incarnation, His perfectly divine and human life, whether we discern this revelation or not.

Therefore, in order to discern God, not merely as an intellectual conception but as a spiritual power and as spiritual life that can affect our own lives, we must have the Spirit of God within us. As we said in a previous study, the Spirit is the microscope of the soul, not enlarging God as the object of our vision but enlarging our capacity of discernment, thus enabling us to see the things of God which cannot be discerned by the natural eye.

It is not necessary for a man to be wicked in his life, a criminal, or a completely selfish person in order to be unspiritual. Even a man of good moral life, in its outward business and social aspects, may be a completely unspiritual man. He cannot see spiritual things because he has not the Spirit of God within him. A moral man finds it hard to see his need of salvation through Christ. He cannot understand that the death of Christ was for the atonement of his sins. As Paul says in 1 Corinthians 2:14, any such doctrine is foolishness to him. "He cannot know it."

That expression in Greek is suggestive of complete innate inability to know. The verb *ou dunatai* means "does not have the dynamic, is incapable of." And the verb translated "know" is *gnōnai*, which refers to acquired knowledge and not the knowledge that is given to man by inspiration. An unconverted man, one not born from above, cannot even see the kingdom of God. Not, of course, that God hides this kingdom from him, but that he lacks that spirit within, akin to the holy and pure Spirit of God, by which he can see the spiritual things of God's kingdom.

But when a man is converted by the Spirit of God, he partakes of this spiritual insight that enables him to discern spiritual things. By their very nature, says Paul, such things can only be discerned spiritually. The word translated "discern" in Greek is *anakrinetai*. This is a composite verb, made up of the preposition *ana*, which intensifies the verb, and the verb *krinō*, which means "to investigate, to distinguish, to judge." *Anakrinetai*, therefore, signifies "to examine, to scrutinize." In modern Greek we use this word to signify the initial investigation of a judge into the possibility of a crime. It is the judicial examination preceding a trial—the first examination, in other words.

The principle that the apostle Paul lays down here is that a spiritual thing can only be judged, examined, scrutinized, by a spiritual instrument. Man born in sin and not born again cannot be in a position to judge the things of the Spirit of God. He cannot even discern the Spirit of God in existence, much less in operation. He cannot discern it at all. It is all one big blur to him. He lacks the ability to distinguish the person of God, the qualities of God, or the acts of God, let alone their meaning in his own individual life.

Paul then goes on to say, "nor can he know." The word "them" does not follow the verb "know" in the Greek text. It is simply, "nor can he know."

How wonderfully, through the Spirit of God, the believer can see the holiness of God, the eternity of God, the infinity of God, the goodness, mercy, and love of God. But how impossible a task this is for the unbeliever. Why does he not say, "But the natural man receives not God," instead of "receives not the things of the Spirit of God"? First of all, it is because the essence of God the Father, God the Son, and God the Holy Spirit, is spirit as distinguished from matter. Second, it is because the transaction between God and man is made between two spirits—God's and man's. Man's spirit is the receiver God originally implanted in him so that he could catch His transmission. It is the Holy Spirit who communicates God in His totality to man. That is what is called the "quickening" of man's spirit by God's Spirit. As Peter said, "for Christ also hath once suffered for sins, the just for the unjust, that he might bring us to God, being put to death in the flesh, but quickened by the Spirit" (1 Pet. 3:18).

Are You Ignorant of Your Ignorance?

Suppose a robbery had been committed in a store in your neighborhood. You join the crowd standing outside and ask, "What happened?" Someone starts to fill you in on what is going on, though he has not been inside the building himself. Then the storekeeper comes out, and you ask the same question. His account differs in many details from that of the bystander. Whom would you believe? The answer is obvious. You realize that the man who stands outside a building is a very poor judge of what is taking place within.

Yet frequently the man who stands outside the circle of born-again Christians refuses to enter or even listen to what is going on inside that circle of those who are in Christ. Unfortunately, when he desires to get information on spiritual things, he does not go to those who have experienced the indwelling of the Spirit of God, but turns to worldly philosophers and rationalists, though outside of the ones spiritually in the know; and therefore the ideas he gets of what is going on inside are totally perverted.

How often one meets young people who say, "I cannot be a Christian because I do not understand what you Christians believe." No wonder, for they have been trying to understand Christian belief by reading the writings of an unbeliever, the natural man who is ignorant of and unable to know the things of the Spirit of God because he himself does not possess that Spirit.

In learning to read, one must start as a child, with the alphabet. There is an ABC of the Christian life, also, and except a man humbles himself to learn it, and becomes a little child, he cannot see the kingdom of God. This is what Christ tells us in Matthew 18:3. The things of God will always be foolishness to the man who does not understand them because he is not spiritually-minded. The man who would interpret Milton to the world must have drunk deeply of the spirit of Milton in order to enter into his thoughts and feelings. The musician who would interpret Handel must have lived with the great composer, so to speak, as his daily companion. Only so can he render the great oratorios faithfully and with sympathy. And the man who would interpret Christ and the things of God must be caught up and taught by the Spirit of God.

Two men were crucified with Christ. One saw only an innocent man cruelly put to death. The other saw the Savior of mankind. It was the same scene but not the same spirit. Scripture teaches that it is the Spirit of God who imparts a change of heart and newness of life to the natural man. God's Spirit within him vitalizes his whole being. It is not mere words; it is a fact rather than a speculation. The individual now realizes the spiritual substance of the gospel, the spiritual power in his heart.

Without the Spirit we cannot understand the Scriptures or the gospel that the Scriptures proclaim. We may understand the doctrines of the gospel but not their spiritual importance for our lives. The Spirit's light is necessary, that the mind and heart may receive the saving influence of the truth. The Holy Spirit must illumine man's spirit in order that the gospel may be realized as a spiritual power. The most accurate exposition of the things of the Spirit will not convey to the heart the power of the gospel without the working of the Spirit upon the heart, anymore than a lively description of the sun will convey to a blind man a true idea of its cheerfulness, warmth, and fructifying power.

It is possible for men to have the gospel upon their lips and not in their hearts. They may know the words but not discern their spiritual meaning. They may apprehend its form as a system but not receive its substance and spirit. They have the letter which killeth but not the spirit which giveth life. A natural man may know the gospel in a formal manner and even be able to expound its doctrine better than a spiritual man. A particular spiritual man may be more deficient in education, slower in comprehension, or more limited in the range of his intellectual grasp than a particular natural man. Nevertheless, the spiritual man has something the natural man does not have. He has a full realization of the gospel and of its power that the natural man fails to comprehend. He possesses the substance while the natural man possesses only the form, the words, the mere morals of the gospel, and not the Spirit that gives life to the gospel.

The spiritual discernment of the gospel does not bring any new revelation to the soul in the sense of showing you something that has not existed before. Neither does it bring new truths not previously revealed. What it does is to bring the old truths home to the soul with new power and personal application. It gives old truths new meaning and light, somewhat different from what was supposed or understood by the natural man. How often newly converted men confess to an entire change, not only in their life, and in the motives and principles of their life, but also in their modes of looking at God and divine things. Everything seems changed to them, everything seems new to them, but it is new to them because they are brought into a new relation of spirit to God and to divine truth. The gospel has a new meaning and purpose, a new attraction to their mind and feeling, so that they can say, "Old things are passed away; behold, all things are become new" (2 Cor. 5:17).

And yet the things were not really new, and old things have not actually passed away, but by spiritual conversion through the working of the Holy Spirit they found themselves with a new attitude to old things; and old things began to wear a new dress and thus became new things to them. As natural men, they did not understand the things of the Spirit and were ignorant of their ignorance, but on becoming spiritual men, they were able to discern the Spirit and spiritual things.

> Lord, I was blind; I could not see
>   In Thy marred visage any grace;
> But now the beauty of Thy face
>   In radiant vision dawns on me.
> Lord, I was dead; I could not stir
>   My lifeless soul to come to Thee;
> But now, since Thou hast quickened me,
>   I rise from sin's dark sepulchre.
> Lord, Thou hast made the blind to see,
>   The deaf to hear, the dumb to speak,
> The dead to live; and lo, I break
>   The chains of my captivity.

What the Holy Spirit Can Do with Your Life

Although we see many evidences of awakened interest in religion today, the application of Christian principles to daily life is often inconsistent and wavering, just as it was in the Corinthian church of Paul's day. That is why Paul had to bring home to them the truth that religious enthusiasm was no substitute for true spirituality. He wanted to teach them the importance of the spiritual mind over that of any other part of their nature.

The natural mind in itself is not sinful by creation. But because of its separation from God in man's fallen condition it functions in a sinful manner. This is why God considers the natural or soulish man as "dead," that is, separated from God and from the spiritual life that is in God. Although the natural man may display a kind of natural goodness, this cannot be compared with the spiritual goodness that is imparted by the Spirit of God. The spiritual life is a better and higher life because it is supernatural in origin. The mind and will and conscience are purified and elevated and enlightened by the Holy Spirit. The spiritual mind is of vastly greater importance in producing the highest forms of manhood and womanhood than anything that can be achieved on the plane of the natural life.

Of course, as there are degrees of development in natural man, there are also degrees of development in spiritual manhood. As some in their natural state know more than others, so in the spiritual life there will be some who have a higher apprehension and appreciation of the things of the Spirit than others. Some will combine in a higher degree the natural qualities of manhood with the spiritual qualities of the soul. Spiritual men with higher natural gifts will always have a wiser and truer appreciation of the purposes and ways of God, and evidence a more profitable and developed conception of spiritual things than do others. They will be less likely to be controlled or tossed about by floods of feeling or passing impulses. However, there is no sameness among spiritual men anymore than there is among natural men, for the gifts of the Spirit are as varied as the gifts of nature.

For this reason we must not regard the moods and feelings of any one man as the determining guide of all spiritual men. We must not regard the spiritual convictions of one man as necessarily and absolutely the true leading of the Spirit for all men, no matter how forcefully he proclaims that his own convictions are the direct teaching of the Spirit. Neither are we to take as the pattern of our spiritual experience the strong impulses and convictions that fill one man in answer to his prayers.

As a rule, the Spirit of God elevates and purifies the natural qualities of our manhood and womanhood, instead of overbearing them or displacing our natural faculties of reason and judgment, thought and intelligence. We are to be no less thoughtful because we are under the influence of the Holy Spirit. We are to be no less wise in our judgment because we have the Spirit of God in us, to help us judge things spiritually discerned. We are not to despise the ordinary sources of intelligence and the enlightened exercise of our reason simply because spiritual things are known and understood only by the Spirit of God. The born-again, Spirit-filled believer is not to abdicate the functions of his reason and will in the normal, everyday decisions of life. We can go too far in that direction, as the woman did who confessed that she expected God to tell her whether to cross the street at every intersection, and would stand immobilized until she thought she had clear leading from Him. Her doctor told her to snap out of such nonsense or she would lose her mind!

The true function of the Holy Spirit is not to set up a new man in real opposition to the natural man, though between the new man and the old man there is a striking contrast. These two, though contrasted in Scripture and in Christian thought, are not of necessity opposed to each other, in that each is a creation of

God. The old man is made new by being made spiritual. The faculties of the natural man are taken up by the Spirit and made spiritual faculties—are influenced spiritually.

As Paul says in 1 Corinthians 1:5, "In everything ye are enriched by him, in all utterance, and in all knowledge." The will we have by nature is renewed; our reason is sanctified; our mind is enlightened; our judgment is purified by the divine influences of the Holy Spirit. In this way our natural man is made spiritual, and we are able to discern spiritual things and to know them. But if we remain natural men and women, relying entirely on our natural faculties, then we cannot receive the things of the Spirit. Indeed, many of them would appear foolish to us because we could not know or understand them. (Simpson 1886, 29:28–30; Williams 1931, 119:282–83).

It is unfortunate that the gospel is sometimes preached today as though all that is involved is one moment of decision. True, the moment of decision is significant. The whole of the rest of the life will be changed because of it. But the point is that nothing less than the whole of the rest of the life is involved. Christianity is not simply a matter of making a decision for Christ. It is a matter of following Him day by day, of realizing in everyday affairs the consequences of the decision once reached. It is a quality of life and a life of quality; we must not settle for less. . . .

The new life in Christ is characterized by the exercise of qualities like love which . . . is the first item in Paul's list of the fruit of the Spirit . . . that love which has been called "the annihilation of the self-seeking life." . . . He who possesses this new life lives his life not in craven fear but in trust in the living God, who redeemed him and who will perfect that which He has begun in him {an editorial writer in *Christianity Today* [August 19, 1966]}.

> If God can make of an ugly seed,
>   With a bit of earth and air
> And dew and rain, sunshine and shade,
>   A flower so wondrous fair,
> What can He make of a soul like you,

With the Bible and faith and prayer
And the Holy Spirit, if you do His will
And trust His love and care?
—Author Unknown

LESSONS:

1. *Psuchikos* is the soulish man. Paul describes this man as being "in Adam"; he is the man estranged from God because of Adam's sin.

2. When one becomes a new creature in Christ Jesus, he is then said to be "in Christ," and he becomes a spiritual being, *pneumatikos*. He is enlivened by the Spirit of God.

3. The soul as distinguished from the spirit cannot know the things of God's Spirit. Only the spirit of man can know anything of the Spirit of God.

4. No one completely lacks the faculty of spiritual perception that belongs essentially to our human nature, but in the natural man it slumbers and only the animal life is awake.

5. A man who has no experimental knowledge of Christ, and who has never felt the sinfulness of sin, is not equipped to pronounce judgment upon the incarnation and the atonement.

6. The Bible clearly teaches that the Creator meant the body for the sake of the soul, and the soul for the sake of the spirit.

7. In the creation of the new man from the old man, the old is not useless; it is preliminary to the new.

8. Spiritual truths can only be discerned by a spiritual mind—a mind aided and strengthened by the higher power of vision that the Spirit of God imparts.

9. Through all life, we discern only that for which we are prepared by the state of our spirit.

10. Paul wanted to bring home to the Corinthians the truth that religious enthusiasm was no substitute for true spirituality. He wanted to teach them the importance of the spiritual mind over that of any other part of their nature.

1 Cor. 2:15 | *How You Can Become a Complete Person*

But he that is spiritual judgeth all things, yet he himself is judged of no man.

Does God Discriminate against Anyone in the Matter of Salvation?

Scripture clearly states that God desires the salvation of all men. "The Lord is . . . not willing that any should perish, but that all should come to repentance" (2 Pet. 3:9). Yet other Scripture verses seem to indicate that He is discriminatory in whom He chooses to reveal Himself. Take 2 Corinthians 4:3, for instance: "But if our gospel be hid, it is hid to them that are lost." True, immediately afterwards in verse 4 Paul says, "In whom the god of this world hath blinded the minds of them which believe not, lest the light of the glorious gospel of Christ, who is the image of God, should shine unto them." Here the blame is squarely placed upon the god of this world, Satan, and upon man's attitude toward God's revelation and truth.

The question is, why does God put His Spirit into some people, enabling them to receive the things of the Spirit of God, to the exclusion of others? If the natural man does not have the innate ability to comprehend the revelation of God, as Paul declares in 1 Corinthians 2:14, then it may be claimed that God's revelation is not universal, since it cannot be appreciated by all men. And if there are those who, by virtue of what they are, cannot appreciate God's revelation, how can they in any sense be held responsible for unwillingness to accept it?

God has sent a message to all men. He desires all men to understand, appreciate, and receive it. But some do not, as Paul says, because they are "natural," soulish, lacking the Spirit of God within. That is a factual observation, but does it do God justice?

God's revelation professes to be given, not to perfect but to imperfect men, not to the holy, but to the sinful who need salvation. On that basis, some might say that Paul's statement in 1 Corinthians 2:15, "But he that is spiritual judgeth all things," is not fair. Why shouldn't the soulish man who needs the Spirit of God be able to discern that which concerns his salvation? After all, the main purpose of the gospel is not to lead upwards that soul who is already on the highway to heaven but to arrest the descent of the sinful soul and lift him from the depths to which he has sunk and is still sinking. Is it fair of God to send His revelation to men who already have spiritual insight, and exclude the person who lacks that insight but desperately needs the grace of God? How are sinners to be saved if the means of salvation cannot reach them because of the very sinfulness from which it is the purpose of the gospel to deliver them?

Before we accuse God of injustice and inequality in His treatment of men, let us examine the matter a bit more carefully. God's revelation was never intended to work mechanically, without regard to the moral action of the person to whom it was offered. It was intended to be effectual only in those who are willing to receive it. It was offered to all, but without the intent to relieve anyone of responsibility for his own life. The responsibility of every person with moral capacities is a fundamental scriptural truth that cannot be set aside. Men are not prevented from accepting the revelation of God by virtue of the fact that they have sinned. Not even the vilest sin can shut out the sinner from the power of believing, provided there still remains a longing for higher things, even though it be of the feeblest sort. But if that longing in the human heart is absolutely gone and cannot be revived, of what value would any revelation be to the soul? Wherever God sees the slightest spark of faith, even in a soul that is in the very darkest depths of evil, His voice will penetrate and touch the heart, clear the insight, and cause the acceptance of His revelation and grace.

The apostle Peter was truly a spiritual man when, responding to the Lord's question, "Whom say ye that I am?" he confessed, "Thou art the Christ, the Son of the living God" (Matt. 16:15, 16). He did not say this because his natural mind had reasoned it out, but because the Spirit of God had revealed it to him. "And Jesus answered and said unto him, Blessed art thou, Simon Barjona: for flesh and blood hath not revealed it unto thee, but my Father which is in heaven" (v. 17). It is as if the Lord were anticipating the words of the apostle Paul, that the spiritual man knows everything, even who Jesus Christ is and what He came to this earth to accomplish in relation to man.

The Lord did not ask this question because He needed to find out what people thought of Him, but He wanted to bring out the truth that God's revelation is given directly by God and is neither discovered by man nor revealed by one man to another. Some soulish men thought that Jesus was Elijah, others that He was the prophet Jeremiah, and so on. But Peter, simply because he had the Spirit of God, was spiritual and therefore knew the truth that the Lord spoke, "Flesh and blood hath not revealed it unto thee, but my Father which is in heaven."

The word translated "blessed" in this verse is the Greek adjective *makarios*, the same word we find in the Beatitudes, which means "characterized by the qualities of deity or indwelt by God." It might well be considered the equivalent of the word "spiritual" that we find in 1 Corinthians 2:15. Because you have God within you, you can recognize God outside of you in the person of the Lord Jesus Christ.

In calling Peter "blessed," the Lord was pointing out that he was highly favored in receiving this revelation from God. Others did not receive it. They tried to reason out who Christ was by their natural thought processes and inferences. That is why they failed to arrive at the truth. You cannot understand God unless you have God within you. Understanding follows receiving Him into your heart and life.

We must understand that God is the author of all knowledge, knowledge that enriches the natural man and also the spiritual man. Natural knowledge, however, can be imparted by mortal men. This is knowledge pertaining to the human arts and sciences. Flesh and blood were designated in Matthew 16:17 as the means of imparting such knowledge. God uses these means as second causes, while He remains the First Cause of all knowledge. He uses natural means to impart natural knowledge, conveying this knowledge indirectly through mortal beings and the laws of nature He has instituted.

But if you have a desire for spiritual knowledge, a desire to receive that revelation of Him that shall transform your thinking and set you on the highway to eternal life, God will never turn you away empty, for Christ Himself has promised, "Blessed are they which do hunger and thirst after righteousness: for they shall be filled" (Matt. 5:6).

Two Kinds of Wisdom

In most of the second chapter of First Corinthians, the apostle Paul discusses the contrast between two kinds of wisdom, wisdom of the natural or psychic man and wisdom of the Spirit. When the apostle says the spiritual man judges or discerns all things, yet he himself is not discerned by any man, he states that the judgments or evaluations of the spiritual man are far superior to those of the natural man in matters relating to God and to man's relationship to Him.

The natural man is unable to discern and to evaluate holiness and the things of the Spirit because they are entirely foreign to him. But the spiritual man, the truly holy man, can understand the natural man and the reason he behaves as he does. He is like one standing on top of a building who can see what is happening below, while it is impossible for the man on the ground to see what is happening on the rooftop. The natural man is of the earth, while the spiritual man stands on higher ground. Because of his position in Christ he can see what is going on below and above, while the natural man cannot comprehend anything above the earthly level.

What are the "all things" that the spiritual man can discern? Some manuscripts translate the word *panta* as "all things" without the definite article *ta*. If the definite article is not there, then *panta* as a collective pronoun would mean not only "the totality of things" but would also have the meaning of *hekastos*, "each one in the totality, every one." Therefore Paul is referring here to the ability of the spiritual person to take life as a whole and analyze it, evaluate it, and discern it, as well as to evaluate each separate situation by itself. Since the spiritual man knows by faith that God governs everything, and that nothing can happen in his life that is not directed by God, he sees a purpose in each individual piece of the puzzle, as it were, and can also visualize the puzzle as a whole with all its individual pieces fitted together. He has the ability to discern the hand of God holding one piece of the puzzle or the entire puzzle made up of all its pieces. This the natural man is unable to do. One of the greatest powers of the spiritual man is to see that the part is indispensable to the whole, though in his finiteness he may not always know where it fits in.

The spiritual man sees the invisible whole and accepts each part with joy.

One of my dearest friends, a Christian brother whom I greatly admired, was Dr. Thomas Lambie. For many years a medical missionary in Abyssinia, he finally died in the Holy Land as he worshiped in the garden tomb on Easter morning. Dr. Lambie used to say that while he was in Africa he learned something very significant from the Africans. They often had to cross bridgeless streams, a difficult procedure because of the danger of being swept off their feet and carried downstream to great depths or hurled to death against the hidden rocks. Dr. Lambie learned from the natives the best way to make such a hazardous crossing. The man about to cross found a large stone, the heavier the better, lifted it to his shoulder, and carried it across the stream as ballast. The extra weight of the stone kept his feet solidly on the bed of the stream so that he could cross safely without being swept away. Even so, the spiritual man regards the heavy stones, the burdens he has to carry in life, not as curses, as the natural man would tend to interpret them, but as steadying influences, as God's provisions enabling him to cross safely to the realm beyond.

Paul maintains in this verse that mere intellect, the soul of man, the wisdom of natural man, is not to be compared with spiritual insight. We must bear in mind, of course, that he is writing to a people brought up in the atmosphere of Greek culture, a culture that attaches the greatest importance to training man's mental powers, and succeeds to an extraordinary degree. It is to such a highly developed Greek-speaking public that Paul addresses himself. To many of them, philosophy is the supreme good, and they can imagine nothing higher. They regard the man of trained, disciplined mind, accustomed to sift, weigh, and judge ideas, as the very height of human excellence, and they look for nothing beyond. But they cannot see there is something that far surpasses the excellence they had attained.

Now here comes Paul, himself learned in all the wisdom of his age and knowing the best that intellect can produce, to upset their complacency. He tells them that there is something higher, to which mere cleverness can give them no access, and which has little or nothing to do with the development of the reasoning faculties. He calls this "the spiritual mind," and maintains that he who possesses it can see the true proportions and inner significance of each thing, each experience, the whole of life, as intellect alone could never do.

What Paul means when he says that the natural man does not accept or know the things of the Spirit of God, whereas the spiritual man discerns each separate thing and all things put together, is what Christ was referring to in those memorable words of Matthew 11:25, 26 when He prayed: "I thank thee, O Father, Lord of heaven and earth, because thou hast hid these things from the wise and prudent, and hast revealed them unto babes. Even so, Father: for so it seemed good in thy sight."

The tale is told of a man who once found his way into an isolated valley inhabited only by blind people. He discovered that no one in the valley had the slightest conception of sight and therefore did not know their own world. They had everything admirably arranged for finding their way about by sense of touch, and were constantly talking about their marvelous achievements in this direction, and what further advances they might achieve in years to come. They ridiculed the visitor's attempts to make them understand what had been revealed to him through the faculty of sight. They did not believe there was any such faculty, and when he persisted in speaking about it they grew angry and began to treat him as a madman.

There was one of these blind folk, however, who finally managed to get some glimmering of what this outsider was trying to tell them, and that was the woman who loved him and whom he loved. Love became an interpreter, even though sight was absent. All the rest were not only unconscious of this, but believed themselves qualified to pass judgment on the man who could see, whereas he was the one who was able to pass judgment on them, for he knew what they did not. Though he could not succeed in imparting his knowledge, he perceived clearly, unerringly, the inadequacy and clumsiness of their way of living as contrasted with what might be if only their eyes could be opened.

This is a perfect illustration of what Paul is trying to teach here, that among other things the spiritual man is able to discern what the natural man lacks, because he knows the things of the Spirit of God, which they do not.

Why the World Cannot Understand the Christian

Some time ago, a young man came to me for counseling because his marriage had broken down after little over a year. He attempted to explain the reason for this in natural causes. However, it was very evident to me that the underlying reason was that he was still what the apostle Paul calls a "natural man," that is, one who had not been born again and was therefore not possessed of the Spirit of God. Because of this he could not understand his wife, who was a spiritual person. Both his wife and I could readily discern what was lacking in his life, though he could not. I had no thought of condemning him, but I could discern where the trouble lay.

This is what our Lord did in the case of the rich young ruler who came to him inquiring about eternal life. "Yet lackest thou one thing," Christ said to him (Luke 18:22). As the born-again man looks at the people of the world, he can discern those in whom the light of the gospel is lacking. He can see that what makes the difference between them and him is the presence of that light within. There is therefore a great deal of difference between the word "judge" and the word "discern." The spiritual man does not judge in the sense of condemning others, but he realizes wherein lies their incompleteness, and hence the source of their difficulties.

This is exactly what the apostle means when he says that the spiritual man discerns each and every "thing"—be it circumstance, event, or person. He is not a know-it-all, but he recognizes and understands the spiritual aspects of life wherever he sees them or finds them lacking.

Paul tells us that spiritual vision is definitely superior to natural intellectual brilliance. He does not despise intellectualism but indicates that spiritual vision alone can give it its true value and place. A person who studies the most interesting aspects of natural life may become so dedicated to intellectualism that he attributes supreme importance to it. It is stimulating to be in the society of very clever people, but it is wiser to seek the company of those who are spiritually-minded. It is a great accomplishment to become an expert in natural science, but it will leave you empty if the spiritual element is missing. Intellect never carries anybody very far on the road to lasting satisfaction and ultimate truth unless it is conjoined to spiritual insight, which is something quite different. Pascal was right when he said, "The heart has its reasons which reason cannot know."

In order to be a complete person, you need the touch of the Eternal, the breath of the divine Spirit, the influx of a life and power not of this world. Is there such a thing? Countless persons who have experienced it testify that there is, though the ordinary man of the world or the intellectual giant may have no cognizance of it and may even scorn the desire for it. No one who has ever felt the power of the Holy Spirit can doubt the fact that this power puts the soul in touch with a higher, vaster sphere in which the things of this world are seen as the shadows, and the things of the Spirit the substance. When you become a spiritual person, the troubles and trials of life assume their proper proportion. All sordidness and baseness are shot through with a radiance that works to purify the heart and vision. Heaven begins here on earth when a person undergoes the change from a natural man to a spiritual man. As a spiritual man he lives consistently with that vision and refuses to allow this world and its ways and values to blind him to the truth (see Campbell 1912, 82:289–91).

Paul goes on to make a statement about the spiritual man that is a little difficult to understand. Not only is he able to discern all things, says Paul, but also "he himself is not judged or discerned by anyone." Does he mean that the spiritual man is so perfect that he can do no wrong, or that the born-again believer is exempt from criticism? No, he is not referring to sinless perfection as an attribute of the Spirit-filled man. I believe the primary meaning here is in harmony with what Paul said in 1 Corinthians 1:8, where he declared, "Who [God] shall also confirm you unto the end, that ye may be blameless in the day of our Lord Jesus Christ."

The word translated "blameless" in this verse is *anenklētous,* which means "without charge or accusation." It is a judicial term, just like the basic noun *krisis,* "judgment," from which the verb *anakrinō* (to make a pre-trial examination) is derived. The believer has a kind of perfection that comes from his being "in Christ." Chapter one of First Corinthians frequently refers to our being "in Christ," meaning that we are positionally perfect in Him because we share His perfection and sinlessness. But in practical life we are not completely sinless, as 1 John 1:8 cautions us: "If we say that we have no sin, we deceive ourselves, and the truth is not in us" (Zodhiates 1972, 117–20).

Thus, the first meaning we must attribute to Paul's statement that the spiritual man is not judged by anyone is that no fellow human being can bring a legal accusation against a believer, as far as his status before God is concerned, because of the very fact that he is "in Christ." The judgment of the believer comes only from the Lord. Interestingly enough, 1 Corinthians 4:3, 4 use the same verb in the Greek text. "But with me," says Paul, "it is a very small thing that I should be judged of you, or of man's judgment: yea, I judge not mine own self. For I know nothing by myself; yet am I not hereby justified: but he that judgeth me is the Lord." Paul recognizes that Christ the Lord is his judge and by extension the sole judge of all born-again believers—as far as their spirituality and the fact that they are in Christ is concerned.

The second meaning of Paul's declaration that the spiritual man is not judged by anyone is that the natural or sensual man cannot understand or appreciate the spiritual man. The natural man may consider him a fool, since natural wisdom considers spiritual wisdom foolishness. "Look what the spiritual man misses!" reasons the natural man. "We enjoy the world, and he deprives himself of so many of its pleasures. What a fool he is to sacrifice so much in this life in the hope of a reward in the future life."

Yes, to live for Christ is foolishness to the natural mind. Self-pleasing is the order of the day, and to most men it is the wisdom of the world. Therefore what the spiritual man is or does cannot be evaluated by the natural man. No natural person, no matter how high his intelligence or how manifold his natural abilities, can truly understand the motives, accomplishments, or philosophy of the spiritual man, the one who is "in Christ."

LESSONS:

1. God's revelation is given directly by God and is neither discovered by man nor revealed by one man to another.

2. Because of his position in Christ, the spiritual man can see what is going on below and above, while the natural man cannot comprehend anything above the earthly level.

3. The spiritual man regards the burdens he has to carry in life, not as curses, as the natural man would tend to interpret them, but as steadying influences, as God's provisions enabling him to cross safely to the realm beyond.

4. Paul is writing to a people brought up in the atmosphere of Greek culture, a culture attaching greatest importance to training man's mental powers, and succeeding to an extraordinary degree.

5. Spiritual vision alone can give intellectualism its true value and place.

1 Cor. 2:16

Being Subject to the Spirit of God

For who hath known the mind of the Lord, that he may instruct him? But we have the mind of Christ.

Is the Christian above the Law?

When the apostle Paul declared that no one can bring legal charges against a Christian to discredit his standing before God, and that no one who is not a believer can judge or understand him aright, he was not declaring that the spiritual man is a law unto himself. Far from it. As the *International Critical Commentary* says, what we have here is "the principle neither of anarchy nor tyranny." In other words, Paul is not suggesting that the Spirit-filled Christian is above all authority, either human or divine. Romans, chapter 13, is very clear concerning the Christian's duty toward the state and its laws. Nor does the Christian become a tyrant when it comes to non-Christians. He is to be subject to their legally constituted rule, though he may never be understood by them.

As the *International Critical Commentary* goes on to say, Paul here:

is not asserting the principle that the individual judgment is for each man the criterion of truth. He is asserting the supremacy of conscience, and the right and duty of personal judgment. It is the spiritual man who has this vantage ground. The text has been perverted in more than one direction; on the one hand, as an excuse for the license of persons whose conduct has stamped them as unspiritual; on the other, as a ground for irresponsibility of ecclesiastical despotism [Robertson and Plummer 1956, 50].

In other words, personal judgment even for the spiritual man cannot be the only criterion of decision and action. There is God's written revelation to consider, as well as the living Christ within him who must reign supreme. It is possible for even the spiritual person to grieve the Holy Spirit by allowing the natural man to spring up in opposition to the spiritual man. A Spirit-filled person, therefore, cannot assume that he is faultless and that his judgment is absolute. It must be made subject to the Spirit of God within, whose leading cannot be contrary to the revealed written Word of God. Nor does Paul's declaration authorize anyone to say, "I am a spiritual leader which gives me the right to impose my will on others, for I cannot be wrong."

First Corinthians 2:16 definitely dismisses any notion that a Christian may have that, because he is in Christ, he knows it all and can be the absolute judge of all things. "For who hath known the mind of the Lord, that he may instruct him [the Lord, that is]? But we have the mind of Christ." What Paul means in brief is that in spite of the fact that we have the mind of Christ—which is synonymous with being spiritual or having the Spirit of God within us—our knowledge of God is only partial and therefore cannot be infallible.

This verse is an interpretative quotation from Isaiah 40:13. I call it that because Paul does not quote the Hebrew text but the Greek Septuagint, and that not with exactness. He did not do this out of ignorance, of course, but with a purpose. The Authorized Version of Isaiah 40:13 reads, "Who hath directed the Spirit of the Lord, or being his counsellor hath taught him?" Paul omits the middle clause here, though he includes it in Romans 11:34. In this latter quotation, however, he omits the final clause.

Why did Paul mention this verse, borrowing the idea at least from Isaiah? In the 12th verse of Isaiah 40, the prophet speaks of the inability of man to measure the waters in the hollow of his hand, or to mete out heaven with the span, or comprehend the dust of the earth in a measure, or weigh the mountains in scales, or the hills in a balance. In other words, Isaiah declares man's inability to measure the physical surroundings of the world he lives in. Presupposing that this physical world was created by the Lord, he says, "Who hath directed the Spirit of the Lord?" In other words, who gave God the wisdom to do all this that man finds himself incapable of even measuring?

The knowledge of God is an integral part of His nature. He is omnipotent, the Creator of all things, and necessarily omniscient. In verse 14 Isaiah goes on to ask, "With whom took he counsel, and who instructed him, and taught him in the path of judgment and taught him knowledge, and showed to him the way of understanding?" The answer, of course, is no one.

When we examine the context of this quotation, we understand why Paul used it in the context of 1 Corinthians 2:16. Paul had spoken of the inability of man's wisdom to understand the depths and mysteries of God, but the person who receives the Spirit of God possesses the One who knows everything since He has created everything. Thus, the Greek text of 1 Corinthians 2:16 reads, "For who knew the mind of the Lord, that he may instruct him?" Paul is referring, of course, to the natural man of whom he spoke in verse 14, who does not receive the things of the Spirit of God because they are foolishness to him, and who cannot know them because they are spiritually discerned.

The first thing that merits attention in verse 16 is the verb *egnō,* translated "hath known" in the Authorized Version. It is exactly the same verb as that in verse 14 in the phrase, "nor can he know them." The verb *ginōskō*, as we explained in previous studies, refers to man's naturally acquired knowledge. It is not the knowledge that man receives by revelation, but the conclusions that he arrives at by his own natural intellectual processes. What Paul is actually saying, then, is that no natural man without the Spirit of God is able to know the mind of God. As human beings we can hardly enter into the mind of a fellow human being, let alone, as finite beings, discover the mind of the infinite God.

The Athenians were being quite honest when they erected altars to the unknown god. They felt that there must be a god different from any they could perceive with their own minds. An ancient historian tells us that at one time a dismal plague visited Athens and, as none of the city's gods seemed able to avert its ravages, Epimenides turned loose a number of sheep and, wherever one of these animals rested, an altar was erected to an unknown God. The people evidently felt their fate was in the hands of one who was not usually worshiped or even recognized in their temples, and wanted to invoke his help. What a true and pathetic picture of human life! The natural man feels that he is in the presence of a power and mystery he cannot understand or control. But the spiritual man can say with Paul, "I know whom I have believed, and am persuaded that he is able to keep that which I have committed unto him against that day" (2 Tim. 1:12).

Who Are You to Question God?

Men often consider God to be unreasonable. That is because the mind of man cannot fathom the mind of God. Not only does the natural man not understand God's Spirit, and therefore does not receive His Spirit, but he also cannot understand why God does what He does. This is why he is often critical of God and rejects the things of the Spirit as foolishness. His mind is inherently incapable of entering into the reasoning processes of God.

When the apostle Paul quoted from Isaiah 40:13, he did so to bring out the point that no natural man—without the Spirit of God—is able to know the mind of God. The Hebrew of Isaiah does not use the word *noun* (accusative case of *nous*), "mind," when referring to the Lord, but speaks instead of "the Spirit of the Lord." In 1 Corinthians 2:16, however, Paul substitutes the phrase "the mind of the Lord," thus equating the two.

Let us examine the meaning of the Greek word *nous*, "mind." Generally speaking, it denotes the seat of reflective consciousness, comprising the faculties of perception, understanding, judging, and determining. In 1 Corinthians 14:14, Paul draws a clear line of distinction in discussing the faculties of the spiritual man that are used if and when he speaks in an unknown tongue.

"For if I pray in an unknown tongue," he says, "my spirit [*pneuma*] prayeth, but my understanding [*nous*] is unfruitful." Here we see the two different faculties of the spiritual man: *pneuma*, "spirit," the faculty of communication with God, and *nous*, "mind," the faculty of reflection or reasoning. Paul now takes his argument one step further. He declares that the natural man cannot even know the reasoning process of God, the mind of God. And the reason he refers to the mind of God is to show that there is really no contradiction between the Spirit of God and the mind of God.

Of course, *nous* denotes more than mere intellect. It denotes also the moral reasoning of God—the "why" of His actions. Who of us will ever know, for instance, why God created the seas and the hills, why He created the ant and the mosquito? It is impossible for us to know these things. But God never did and never does and never will do anything without some moral reason or purpose.

The word for "Lord" in Greek is *kuriou,* the equivalent for Jehovah in the Old Testament. *Kurios* in Greek means "the strong one." The meaning, therefore, of the question that Paul asks in 1 Corinthians 2:16 is, "For who ever knew the mind, the reason, of the Strong One?" Sometimes strength acts out of caprice. A strong man may do things for no other purpose or reason than to demonstrate his strength. This is not so with God. The Strong One has a mind, and this infuses a moral purposefulness into all the demonstrations of the strength of God. Logically, if anyone were able to know the mind of God, he would be equal with God or even superior to Him and would be able to instruct Him. That is why Paul adds, "For who has ever known the mind of the Lord? Who shall instruct him?" The word "him" here should be capitalized, for it refers to the Lord of the previous phrase. The verb translated "instruct" is *sumbibasei* in Greek, which comes from the conjunction *sun,* meaning "with," and the verb *bibazō,* meaning "to lift up." Literally it means "to lift up together, to join, or to knit," and therefore "to instruct." The etymological meaning of the word, however, is "to bring about an agreement," and it is used in this sense even in modern Greek. You instruct two people so that you may bring about an agreement between them.

If the natural man, Paul argues, were capable of knowing the moral reasoning of God, he could instruct God accordingly. He could correct God and tell Him how to do His work better. Is it not true that the natural man in his attitude toward God often thinks within himself, "If I were God I would have done thus and so"? Even Christians sometimes are tempted to feel that way, when they wonder why God permits certain things in their lives. The reason you react this way is because you do not know the mind, the reasoning, of God and what He is trying to accomplish by what He is doing. Not having the Spirit of God—or not being fully yielded to that Spirit—you cannot know God's purpose and reasoning.

But then Paul adds a triumphant note. "But we have the mind of Christ." He makes an important point here in changing the word "Lord" to the word "Christ" in this verse. Of course the word "we" refers to the apostle Paul and all believers, those who have received the Spirit of God. Why does Paul say that we, the saints of God who have received Jesus Christ as our Savior, have the Spirit of Christ rather than the Spirit of the Lord? Because he wants his readers to understand that Christ *has* the Spirit of the Lord, that He *is* the Lord, and that He *knows* the Lord, being equal with Him and co-eternal with Him. Therefore, if we have the mind of Christ, we also automatically have the mind of God. The apostle here equates the mind of the Lord with the mind of Christ.

Furthermore, Paul wants to indicate that the only way in which we can know God is through the Lord Jesus Christ, by receiving Him into our hearts as Savior and Lord. Christ Himself clearly equated Himself with the Father when He said, "If ye had known me, ye should have known my Father also: and from henceforth ye know him, and have seen him" (John 14:7).

Paul does not say that we *know* the mind of God or that we can explain all the moral reasons of God. This is not true even of the believer, the spiritual man. I for one do not know why God does all that He does in the world today, nor can I find out. But I know God, and therefore I accept His actions by faith, knowing that God as a loving Father does all things well, and I am never to question His wisdom. This is why Paul tells us we have the mind of Christ. Not that we know all that Christ knows, but we have His mind, and therefore by faith we accept His reasoning and purposes as resulting in the best possible actions by an omniscient and omnipotent God.

> I know not, but God knows;
>   Oh, blessed rest from fear!
> All my unfolding days
>   Each anxious, puzzled "why?"
> From doubt or dread that grows,
>   Finds answer in this thought:
> I know not, but He knows.
>   —Annie Johnson Flint

What It Means To Have the Mind of Christ

Man has always wondered about the reasons behind what God does, or permits to happen, in this world. Why does He snatch a little child away from his parents? Why does He permit an accident resulting in the death of thousands? Why does He allow plagues? Why does He permit tyrants to torture innocent people—including those who believe in and trust Him? The apostle Paul tells us that man with his natural intelligence cannot see the moral reasoning behind God's actions, either individually or collectively. Even the spiritual man cannot do this.

"For who hath known the mind of the Lord, that he may instruct him?" Paul asks. Then he adds, "But we have the mind of Christ." It is interesting to note that the definite article does not appear before the Greek word *noun*, "mind," either in the first part of this verse or the last. Paul does not ask, "But whoever knew *the* mind of the Lord?" but "Who knows the mind of the Lord, or the Lord's mind?"—which would indicate not the sum total of God's intelligence, but rather the workings and expression of that intelligence.

It would have been a redundant truth if Paul had stated simply that the natural man cannot know the totality of God's intelligence. This is a self-evident fact that everybody recognizes. The finite cannot see the infinite in its entirety, even as the part cannot see the whole, since it is always smaller than the whole.

Natural intelligence finds no explanation in the acts of God as the product of reason.

Nevertheless, says Paul, "We have Christ's mind." By this he does not mean that we, as spiritual people who by God's grace have made the decision to receive Christ as Savior, have received the total intelligence of Christ and are therefore equal in power and wisdom to Him. There can be no equality between the believer and the Lord Jesus Christ. In a miraculous way Christ comes to dwell in our hearts. We have Christ when we are in Christ. As Peter says, we are "partakers of the divine nature" (2 Pet. 1:4). This does not mean, however, that God in His entirety is confined within or limited to the space of our own personalities. Even as I am indwelt by the Spirit of God, so are millions of others, without in any way limiting the objective entity of the mind of Christ or the Spirit of Christ.

Christ is infinite, and in one respect we can liken Him to the ocean. I can bring my cup and fill it to the brim with ocean water, but I certainly cannot hold all the ocean in my cup. Christ is our possession, but not exclusively so, nor do we have so much of Christ that we may not have a refill of Him or of His Spirit. When Paul admonishes the Ephesians, "Be filled with the Spirit" (Eph. 5:18), he uses the same tense of the verb that he does in 1 Corinthians 2:16. It is not the aorist, which would indicate a once-and-for-all filling, but it is *plērousthe,* "be continuously or repeatedly filled." Interestingly, what is translated as "the Spirit" is simply "Spirit" without the definite article. Again the idea is that you cannot contain all the Spirit of God nor can you receive Him all at once. Somehow, neither Christ nor the Spirit of God nor the mind of Christ becomes static or stale in the believer. It is to Christians, spiritual persons, that Paul writes in Romans 12:2, "And be not conformed to this world: but be ye transformed by the renewing of your mind [*nŏs,* genitive, the same word as used in 1 Cor. 2:16], that ye may prove what is that good, and acceptable, and perfect will of God." There will always be a need for constant renewing of our mind which is the mind of Christ, and a constant need for the infilling of the Holy Spirit.

Observe, furthermore, the certainty with which Paul states that believers possess the mind of Christ. He says, "We have," not "We think we have," or "We feel we have," but "We have." This mind of Christ is within our possession. And since we have the mind of Christ, then we are in full agreement with Him. You recall the meaning of the word *sumbibasei* in the second phrase of our verse, translated "instructing"? It means "to bring up together, to knit." This is exactly what happens when we have the mind of Christ. We are brought into full agreement with and acceptance of all that God does. Since His wisdom becomes our wisdom, our wisdom then agrees with His, and we are reconciled as to life and purpose.

Paul does not say here that as spiritual beings we can understand all that God does or permits, but having His mind we accept it all and will rejoice over it all. "And we know that all things work together for good to them that love God, to them who are the called according to his purpose" (Rom. 8:28). Even in this verse Paul does not say how things work; he simply states the final purpose of these occurrences in our lives, which is the glory of God and our own good as perceived by God in terms of eternity.

One more lesson from this declaration by the apostle Paul: having the mind of Christ does not mean that we lose our own individual natural intelligence. When a person becomes a Christian, his IQ does not necessarily change, but he receives the ability to accept the intelligence of God, and thus his own intelligence cooperates with God. He becomes God's active co-worker. When you become a spiritual person, your personality is not destroyed or even impaired by your yielding to the control of Him who holds its secret key. On the contrary, it is developed to its maximum possibility, until your life in its every part makes its full contribution to God's glory in the world.

J. Stuart Holden gives a beautiful illustration of this. He says,

> I have around my home a garden. In that garden and its possibilities I have the mind of nature. For instance, I know what soil and what seed should produce this, that, and all the other kinds of flowers and fruit; I see set forth in the seedsmen's catalogues the wonderful things that the garden should bring forth.... But mark you, the flowers and the fruit are only produced by labor, by obedience to the laws of nature. And when the garden has been made beautiful and fruitful, it has been made so only by intelligent cooperation with nature. Similarly, we Christians have the mind of Christ. We know full well what a Christian life should be.

But the fruits of the Spirit are only made evident in our lives as we wholeheartedly cooperate with the Lord in full submission and obedience to Him, by letting His Spirit have full control of us—body, soul and spirit.

LESSONS:

1. A Spirit-filled person's judgment must be subject to the Spirit of God within, whose leading is not contrary to the revealed written Word of God.

2. Although we have the mind of Christ, our knowledge of God is only partial, and therefore cannot be infallible.

3. In 1 Corinthians 2:16, the apostle Paul quotes from Isaiah 40:13 to point out that no natural man is able to know the mind of God.

4. Christ is our possession, but not exclusively so, nor do we have so much of Christ that we may not have a refill of Him or of His Spirit.

5. When we have the mind of Christ, we are brought into full agreement with and acceptance of all that God does. Since His wisdom becomes our wisdom, our wisdom then agrees with His, and we are reconciled as to life and purpose.

Bibliography

Alexander, Archibald. "The Hidden Ways of God's Wisdom." In *Christian World Pulpit* 117(1930): 87, 88.

Allon, Henry. "The Dominion of Faith." In *Christian World Pulpit* 33 (1888): 136–37.

Anderson, George Wood. *Unfinished Rainbows.* New York: The Abingdon Press, 1922.

Arnot, William. *Laws from Heaven for Life on Earth* (Illustrations from the Book of Proverbs, First Series). Edinburgh: T. Nelson & Sons, 1856.

Beecher, H. W. *Sermons.* vol. 1. New York: Harper & Brothers, 1868.

Beveridge, William. *Bishop Beveridge's Works.* vol. 2. London: James Duncan and G. & W. B. Whittaker, 1824.

Campbell, R. J. "Spiritual Discernment." In *Christian World Pulpit* 82 (1912): 289–91.

Chafer, Lewis Sperry. *He That Is Spiritual.* Chicago: The Bible Institute Colportage Association, 1929.

Chown, J. P. "Future Glory Revealed." In *Christian World Pulpit* 12 (1877): 273–76.

Davies, A. E. "St. Paul at Corinth." In *Christian World Pulpit* 136 (1939): 182–87.

Dixon, A. C. *Through Night to Morning.* New York: George H. Doran Company, n.d.

Farmer, Herbert H. *Things Not Seen.* London: Nisbet & Co., 1927.

Georgeson, Fred H. "Pulpit Oratory." In *Christian World Pulpit* 71 (1907): 194, 195.

Greenhough, J. G. *The Mind of Christ in St. Paul.* London: Hodder and Stoughton, n.d.

Hanson, George. "The Unique Gospel." In *Christian World Pulpit* 80 (1911): 150–52.

Hastings, James., ed. *The Great Texts of the Bible: Ephesians to Colossians.* Edinburgh: T. & T. Clark, 1913.

Horton, Robert F. *The Trinity.* London: Horace Marshall & Son. 1901.

James, D. Ewart. "Things Which God Hath Prepared." In *Christian World Pulpit* 110 (1926): 220–22.

Jones, J. D. *The Hope of the Gospel.* London: Hodder and Stoughton Ltd., 1926.

Kittel, Gerhard, ed. *Theological Dictionary of the New Testament.* vol. 1. Grand Rapids, MI: Wm. B. Eerdmans Publishing Company, 1964.

_____. *Ibid.,* vol. 3. 1965.

_____. *Ibid.,* vol.4. 1967.

Leyland, A. W. "The Strength of the Weak." In *Christian World Pulpit* 119 (1931) 78.

Maclaren, Alexander. *A Rosary of Christian Graces.* London: Horace Marshall & Son, 1903.

Meyer, F. B. *The Soul s Ascent.* London: Horace Marshall & Son, 1901.

Miller, J. R. *A Message for the Day.* 2nd ed. London: Hodder and Stoughton, 1897.

Morgan, G. Campbell. *The Westminster Pulpit.* vol. 9. Old Tappan, New Jersey: Fleming H. Revell Company, 1955.

Morrison, George. *The Afterglow of God.* New York or London: Hodder and Stoughton, 1912.

Neale, J. M. *Sermons Preached in Sackville Conege Chapel.* vol. 2. London: J. Masters and Company, 1875.

Parker, Joseph. *Preaching Through the Bible.* vol. 26. Grand Rapids, MI: Baker Book House, 1959.

Robertson, Archibald, and Plummer, Alfred. "A Critical and Exegetical Commentary on the Epistle of St. Paul to the Corinthians." In *International Critical Commentary* (1956): 50.

Selby, Thomas G. *The Imperfect Angel and Other Sermons.* 2d ed. London: Hodder and Stoughton, 1889.

Simpson, William. "Discerning Spiritual Things." In *Christian World Pulpit* 29 (1886): 28–30.

Smeaton, George. *The Doctrine of the Holy Spirit.* London: The Banner of Truth Trust, 1958.

South, Robert. "Christianity Mysterious, and the Wisdom of God in Making It So." *Sermons by Robert South.* vol. 1. London: H. G. Bohn, 1855.

Thomas, Reuen. "Natural Man and the Spiritual." In *Christian World Pulpit* 44 (1893): 113–15.

Vinet, Alexander. "The Mysteries of Christianity." In *The World's Great Sermons,* compiled by Grenville Kleiser, vol. 4. New York: Funk &

Wagnalls Company, 1908.

Watkinson, William L. *The Duty of Imperial Thinking*. New York: Fleming H. Revell Company, 1906.

————. *Life's Unexpected Issues*. London: Cassell and Company, Ltd., 1912.

Westcott, Bishop. "The Christian Idea of the Unseen." In *The Anglican Pulpit Library* 12 (n.d.): 89–94.

Williams, J. W. Huxley. "The Spiritual Faculty." In *Christian World Pulpit* 119 (1931): 282–83.

Young, Dinsdale T. *The Crimson Book*. Cincinnati, OH: Jennings and Graham, 1903.

Youngdahl, Reuben K. *The Secret of Greatness*. Westwood, NJ: Fleming H. Revell Co., 1955.

Lexicons, Encyclopedias, and References for Greek Readers, from Classical and Koine Greek to Modern Greek

Byzantiou, S. D. *Lexikon tēs Hellēnikēs Glōssēs (Lexicon of the Hellenic Language)*. Athens: Koromēla, A., 1852.

Dēmētrakou, D. *Lexikon tēs Hellēnikēs Glōssēs (Lexicon of the Hellenic Language)*. Athens: Dēmētrakou, 1954.

Enkuklopaidikon Glōssologikon Lexikon (Encyclopedic Glossological Lexicon). Athens: Morfōtikē Hetaireia.

Enkuklopaidikon Lexikon Eleutheroudaki (Eleutheroudaki Encyclopedic Lexicon). Athens: Eleutheroudakis, 1927.

Kalaraki, Michael and Nikolas Galanos. *Iōannou tou Chrusostomou Ta Hapanta (Complete Works of John Chrysostom)*, 1899.

Liddell, Henry George, and Robert Scott. *Greek–English Lexicon*, as Translated and Enriched by Xenophōn P. Moschos and Michael Kōnstantinides. Athens: John Sideris.

Megalē Helēnikē Enkuklopaideia (Great Hellenic Encyclopedia). Pursos (Pyrsos), Athens: Hēlios.

Neōteron Enkuklopaidikon Lexikon Hēliou (New Encyclopedic Lexicon "Hēlios"). Athens: Hēlios.

Papaoikonomou, George L. *Lexikon Anōmalōn Rhēmatōn (Lexicon of Irregular Verbs)*. Athens: Kagiaphas.

Stamatakou, J. D., *Lexikon Archaias Hellēnikēs Glōssēs* (*Lexicon of the Ancient Hellenic Language*). Athens: Petrou Dēmētrakou, 1949.

Works by Spiros Zodhiates

Conquering the Fear of Death. Grand Rapids, MI: Wm. B. Eerdmans Publishing Co., 1970.

A Richer Life for You in Christ. Ridgefield, NJ: AMG Publishers, 1972.

Was Christ God? Grand Rapids, MI: Wm. B. Eerdmans Publishing Company, 1970.

Scripture Index